Grundschulwörterbuch Englisch

Langenscheidt

Autorin: Karen Richardson
Zeichnungen: Hans-Jürgen Feldhaus

Umwelthinweis: Gedruckt auf chlorfrei gebleichtem Papier
Titelgestaltung: Independent Medien-Design unter Verwendung von
Zeichnungen von Hans-Jürgen Feldhaus

© 2003 by Langenscheidt KG, Berlin und München
Druck: J. P. Himmer, Augsburg
Printed in Germany
ISBN 3-468-20410-8 für die Hardcover-Ausgabe
ISBN 3-468-20415-9 für die broschierte Ausgabe
www.langenscheidt.de

Einleitung

Liebe Schülerin, lieber Schüler,

Englisch lernen – mit deinem neuen Grundschulwörterbuch Englisch ist das ganz einfach!
Und so kann das Grundschulwörterbuch dir beim Lernen helfen:
Such dir zunächst aus den 20 verschiedenen Themen eins heraus und schau dir dazu in Ruhe das Wimmelbild an. Hier kannst du schon viele interessante Sachen entdecken und zu einigen bereits die englische Bezeichnung. Lies dann die einzelnen englischen Wörter zu diesem Themenbereich mit der deutschen Übersetzung. Versuch, dir das englische Wort zu merken. Das kleine Bild neben dem Wort hilft dir sicher dabei.
Der Beispielsatz zeigt dir dann, wie man das englische Wort richtig anwendet. Wenn du den Satz nicht gleich verstehst, so schau dir noch mal das große Bild an. Hier findest du alles wieder, was mit den Sätzen ausgedrückt wird. Noch mehr Informationen gibt es manchmal in kleinen Kästchen, die z.B. Wochentage und Monate oder wichtige Fragen und Antworten enthalten. Im Kapitel Schule stehen im Kästchen Arbeitsanweisungen, die du im Unterricht sicher oft hören wirst.
Wenn du nicht weißt, zu welchem Thema ein Wort gehört, kannst du es im Verzeichnis am Ende des Buches schnell nachschlagen. Hier findest du auch die Lautschrift zu den englischen Wörtern, damit du weißt, wie du sie richtig aussprechen musst.

Und nun wünschen wir dir viel Spaß beim Englischlernen.

Autorin und Verlag

Inhaltsverzeichnis

1 My family and friends — 6

2 My home — 14

3 My room, my toys — 22

4 My body — 28

5 Feelings — 36

6 Clothes — 44

7 My day — 52

8 At school — 60

9 Hobbies and sports — 70

10 Food and drink — 76

11 Shopping — 84

12	In the town	90
13	On the farm	98
14	At the zoo	104
15	At the fairground	112
16	Around the year	118
17	On holiday	126
18	Birthday	134
19	Christmas	140
20	Opposites, numbers, colours, shapes and prepositions	148
	Wörterverzeichnis Englisch-Deutsch	154
	Wörterverzeichnis Deutsch-Englisch	166

My family and friends

grandmother

grandfather

friend

father

tortoise

girl

beard

mother

glasses

dog

baby

boy

cat

My family and friends

am bin
I am eleven years old.
Ich bin elf Jahre alt.

---

are sind
Holly and Jack
are my best friends.
Holly und Jack
sind meine besten
Freunde.

---

aunt die Tante
Aunt Lizzie is
Uncle Bill's wife.
Tante Lizzie ist
Onkel Bills Frau.

---

baby das Baby
Aunt Lizzie, Uncle Bill
and the **baby** live
on a farm.
Tante Lizzie, Onkel Bill
und das Baby wohnen
auf einem Bauernhof.

---

to be sein
It's fun **to be** a child.
Es macht Spaß,
ein Kind zu sein.

beard der Bart
Uncle Bill has a **beard**.
Onkel Bill hat einen Bart.

---

best beste, bester
Who is your **best** friend?
Wer ist dein bester Freund?

---

boy der Junge
Bist du ein
Junge oder
ein Mädchen?

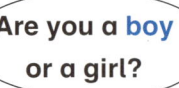

Are you a boy or a girl?

---

brother der Bruder
Max is my **brother**.
Max ist mein Bruder.

---

to be called heißen
The farm cat
is **called**
Winston.
Der Kater vom Bauernhof
heißt Winston.

---

cat die Katze, der Kater
The baby likes
the **cat**.
Das Baby mag
die Katze.

8

My family and friends

child das Kind
Aunt Lizzie has one child.
Tante Lizzie hat ein Kind.

Dad Papa
This is my dad.
Das ist mein Papa.

children die Kinder
There are two children in the tree.
Im Baum sitzen zwei Kinder.

daughter die Tochter
My mum has two daughters.
Meine Mama hat zwei Töchter.

to climb klettern
Max and Mia have climbed up the tree.
Max und Mia sind auf den Baum geklettert.

dog der Hund
Queenie is my dog.
Queenie ist mein Hund.

England England
We live in England.
Wir wohnen in England.

to come from kommen aus
I come from England.
Ich komme aus England.

English Englisch
We speak English.
Wir sprechen Englisch.

cousin der Cousin, die Cousine
The baby is my cousin.
Das Baby ist mein Cousin.

family die Familie
This is my family.
Das ist meine Familie.

My family and friends

father der Vater
Grandpa is Dad's father.
Opa ist Papas Vater.

fine gut
I'm fine, thanks.
Mir geht's gut, danke.

friend der Freund, die Freundin
The cat is the baby's best friend.
Der beste Freund des Babys ist die Katze.

German Deutsch
Can you speak German?
Kannst du Deutsch sprechen?

girl das Mädchen
I'm a girl, Max is a boy.
Ich bin ein Mädchen, Max ist ein Junge.

glasses die Brille
Mum wears reading glasses.
Mama trägt eine Lesebrille.

grandfather der Großvater
I call my grandfather Grandpa.
Ich nenne meinen Großvater Opa.

grandmother die Großmutter
I call my grandmother Grandma.
Ich nenne meine Großmutter Oma.

grandparents die Großeltern
Grandpa and Grandma are my grandparents.
Opa und Oma sind meine Großeltern.

to have haben
I have a big family.
Ich habe eine große Familie.

My family and friends

hello hallo
Hello, my name is Mia.
Hallo, mein Name ist Mia.

mother die Mutter
Grandma is Dad's mother.
Oma ist Papas Mutter.

hi hallo, hi
Hi, I'm Max.
Hi, ich bin Max.

mum Mama
This is my mum.
Das ist meine Mama.

husband der Ehemann
Dad is Mum's husband.
Papa ist Mamas Ehemann.

my mein
My grandparents like to dance.
Meine Großeltern tanzen gern.

is ist
The baby is one year old.
Das Baby ist ein Jahr alt.

name der Name
Hello, my name is Penny.
Hallo, mein Name ist Penny.

man der Mann
Dad is a man. Uncle Bill is a man, too.
Papa ist ein Mann. Onkel Bill ist auch ein Mann.

parents die Eltern
Mum and Dad are our parents.
Mama und Papa sind unsere Eltern.

pet das Haustier
I have a pet.
Ich habe ein Haustier.

My family and friends

photo das Foto
This is my favourite photo.
Dies ist mein Lieblingsfoto.

this dies
This is Buttercup.
Dies ist Buttercup.

pilot der Pilot
My dad is a pilot.
Mein Papa ist Pilot.

too auch
The cat lives on the farm, too.
Die Katze wohnt auch auf dem Bauernhof.

to read lesen
Mum loves to read.
Mama liest gern.

tortoise die Schildkröte
Grandma has a tortoise called Lady Slow.
Oma hat eine Schildkröte namens Lady Slow.

sister die Schwester
Mia is my sister.
Mia ist meine Schwester.

son der Sohn
The baby is Aunt Lizzie's son.
Das Baby ist Tante Lizzies Sohn.

twins die Zwillinge
Max and Mia are twins.
Max und Mia sind Zwillinge.

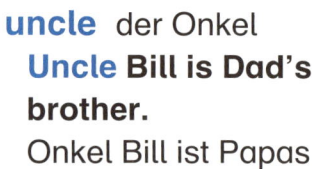

to speak sprechen
Can you speak English, too?
Kannst du auch Englisch sprechen?

uncle der Onkel
Uncle Bill is Dad's brother.
Onkel Bill ist Papas Bruder.

My family and friends

uniform die Uniform
Dad is wearing his dark blue pilot's **uniform**.
Papa trägt seine dunkelblaue Pilotenuniform.

woman die Frau
Mum is a woman. Aunt Lizzie is a **woman**, too.
Mama ist eine Frau. Tante Lizzie ist auch eine Frau.

wife die Ehefrau
Uncle Bill has a **wife**.
Onkel Bill hat eine Frau.

years old ... Jahre alt
The twins are nine **years old**.
Die Zwillinge sind neun Jahre alt.

Questions and answers	Fragen und Antworten
Where do you come from? Woher kommst du?	**I come from England.** Ich komme aus England.
Where do you live? Wo wohnst du?	**I live in London.** Ich wohne in London.
What's your name? Wie ist dein Name?	**My name is Penny.** Mein Name ist Penny.
How old are you? Wie alt bist du?	**I'm eleven.** Ich bin elf.
Do you have a brother? Hast du einen Bruder?	**Yes, I have a brother and a sister.** Ja, ich habe einen Bruder und eine Schwester.
Do you have a pet? Hast du ein Haustier?	**Yes, I have a dog.** Ja, ich habe einen Hund.
How are you? Wie geht es dir?	**I'm fine, thanks.** Mir geht's gut, danke.

squirrel

tree house

My home

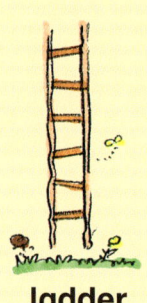
ladder

television

armchair

curtain   toilet paper   spider   bush   bee

My home

address die Adresse
  What's your address?
  Wie ist deine Adresse?

---

apartment (AE) die Wohnung
  Do you live in a house or in an apartment?
  Wohnst du in einem Haus oder in einer Wohnung?

---

armchair der Sessel
  Queenie likes to sleep on the armchair
  Queenie schläft gern auf dem Sessel.

---

at home zu Hause
  Everybody is at home today.
  Heute sind alle zu Hause.

---

attic der Dachboden
  Mum is looking for a book in the attic.
  Mama sucht ein Buch auf dem Dachboden.

---

balcony der Balkon
  My teacher has lots of flowers on her balcony.
  Meine Lehrerin hat viele Blumen auf ihrem Balkon.

---

bath die Badewanne
  The yellow duck is sitting on the bath.
  Die gelbe Ente sitzt auf der Badewanne.

---

bathroom das Badezimmer
  Who is in the bathroom?
  Wer ist im Badezimmer?

---

bedroom das Schlafzimmer
  I'm in my bedroom.
  Ich bin in meinem Schlafzimmer.

---

bee die Biene
  The bee is flying around the rose bush.
  Die Biene fliegt um den Rosenbusch.

My home

bird house das Vogelhäuschen
  Can you see the robin in the bird house?
  Kannst du das Rotkehlchen im Vogelhäuschen sehen?

bush der Busch
  The bee loves the rose bush.
  Die Biene liebt den Rosenbusch.

can können
  Can you see the mouse in the kitchen?
  Kannst du die Maus in der Küche sehen?

carpet der Teppich
  I like the carpet in the hall.
  Ich mag den Teppich im Flur.

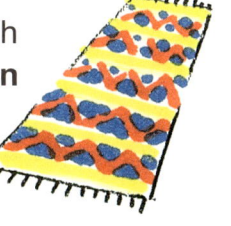

cellar der Keller
  Queenie doesn't like the cellar.
  Queenie mag den Keller nicht.

chimney der Schornstein
  The bird is sitting on the chimney.
  Der Vogel sitzt auf dem Schornstein.

countryside das Land, die Landschaft
  Aunt Lizzie and Uncle Bill live in the countryside.
  Tante Lizzie und Onkel Bill wohnen auf dem Land.

curtain der Vorhang
  Who is hiding behind the curtain?
  Wer versteckt sich hinter dem Vorhang?

dining room das Esszimmer
  Our neighbours eat their dinner in their dining room.
  Unsere Nachbarn essen in ihrem Esszimmer zu Abend.

My home

door die Tür
Our house has a big blue door.
Unser Haus hat eine große blaue Tür.

garage die Garage
The car and the bicycles are in the garage.
Das Auto und die Fahrräder sind in der Garage.

downstairs unten
Grandma and Grandpa are downstairs.
Oma und Opa sind unten.

garden der Garten
The twins are playing in the garden.
Die Zwillinge spielen im Garten.

flat die Wohnung
We live in a house. My teacher lives in a flat.
Wir wohnen in einem Haus. Meine Lehrerin wohnt in einer Wohnung.

grass das Gras
Queenie doesn't like to sit on the wet grass.
Queenie sitzt nicht gern im nassen Gras.

flower die Blume
There are lots of flowers in the garden.
Es gibt viele Blumen im Garten.

hairbrush die Haarbürste
Where is my hairbrush?
Wo ist meine Haarbürste?

front door die Haustür
Dad is at the front door.
Papa steht vor der Haustür.

My home

hall der Flur
The umbrellas are in the hall.
Die Regenschirme sind im Flur.

house das Haus
We live in a red house.
Wir wohnen in einem roten Haus.

key der Schlüssel
Dad is looking for his key.
Papa sucht seinen Schlüssel.

kitchen die Küche
The mouse is in the kitchen looking for the cheese.
Die Maus ist in der Küche und sucht nach Käse.

ladder die Leiter
Climb the ladder up to the tree house.
Kletter die Leiter zum Baumhaus hoch.

to live wohnen, leben
Do you live in a house or a flat?
Wohnst du in einem Haus oder in einer Wohnung?

living room das Wohnzimmer
Grandpa and Grandma are dancing in the living room.
Opa und Oma tanzen im Wohnzimmer.

to look for suchen
Queenie is looking for her bone.
Queenie sucht ihren Knochen.

neighbour der Nachbar
Rita and Sanjay are our neighbours.
Rita und Sanjay sind unsere Nachbarn.

roof das Dach
There is a chimney on the roof.
Es gibt einen Schornstein auf dem Dach.

My home

rose die Rose
Red roses are Mum's favourite flowers.
Rote Rosen sind Mamas Lieblingsblumen.

shampoo das Shampoo
I wash my hair with the green shampoo.
Ich wasche meine Haare mit dem grünen Shampoo.

shed der Schuppen
Mia's in the shed.
Mia ist im Schuppen.

shower die Dusche
Dad likes to have a hot shower on cold mornings.
Papa mag eine heiße Dusche an kalten Morgen.

sink das Waschbecken
There is a lot of water in the sink.
Da ist viel Wasser im Waschbecken.

soap die Seife
Max doesn't like soap.
Max mag keine Seife.

sofa das Sofa
Mum likes to read on the sofa.
Mama liest gern auf dem Sofa.

spider die Spinne
The spider is in the bath.
Die Spinne ist in der Badewanne.

squirrel das Eichhörnchen
The squirrel is angry with Max.
Das Eichhörnchen ist wütend auf Max.

stairs die Treppe
Don't fall down the stairs!
Fall nicht die Treppe runter!

My home

tap der Wasserhahn
The cold tap is blue, and the hot tap is red.
Der Kaltwasserhahn ist blau, der Warmwasserhahn ist rot.

towel das Handtuch
The towels are hanging next to the sink.
Die Handtücher hängen neben dem Waschbecken.

telephone das Telefon
The telephone is on a table in the hall.
Das Telefon steht auf einem Tisch im Flur.

tree der Baum
There's a big old tree in the garden.
Im Garten steht ein großer alter Baum.

television der Fernseher
After school I watch television with the twins.
Nach der Schule sehe ich mit den Zwillingen fern.

treehouse das Baumhaus
Max is in the treehouse.
Max ist im Baumhaus.

toilet die Toilette
Queenie! Don't drink out of the toilet.
Queenie! Nicht aus der Toilette trinken.

upstairs oben
My bedroom is upstairs.
Mein Zimmer ist oben.

toilet paper das Toilettenpapier
Help! Where's the toilet paper?
Hilfe! Wo ist das Toilettenpapier?

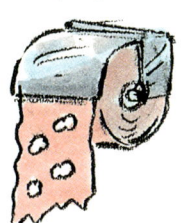

My room, my toys

doll

tennis racket

ball

comic

box

game

keyboard

poster

lamp

mobile phone

chair

dice   alarm clock piggy bank  radio

My room, my toys

alarm clock der Wecker
My alarm clock is very loud.
Mein Wecker ist sehr laut.

cassette die Kassette
My cassettes are on the shelf.
Meine Kassetten sind auf dem Regal.

ball der Ball
Why is Max's ball in my room?
Warum ist Max' Ball in meinem Zimmer?

CD die CD
This is my favourite CD.
Dies ist meine Lieblings-CD.

bed das Bett
I like to stay in bed on rainy days.
Ich bleibe an Regentagen gern im Bett.

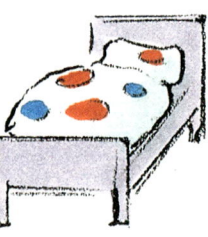

CD player der CD-Player
My music CDs are next to the CD player.
Meine CDs sind neben dem CD-Player.

box die Schachtel
How many boxes are on the shelf?
Wie viele Schachteln sind auf dem Regal?

chair der Stuhl
Do you like my blue chair?
Magst du meinen blauen Stuhl?

to break kaputtmachen
Be careful! Don't break the piggy bank.
Sei vorsichtig! Mach das Sparschwein nicht kaputt.

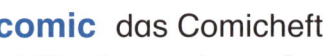

comic das Comicheft
I like to read comics in bed.
Ich lese gern Comichefte im Bett.

My room, my toys

computer der Computer
Sometimes I do my homework on the computer.
Manchmal mache ich meine Hausaufgaben am Computer.

dinosaur der Dinosaurier
Rex, the dinosaur, is on top of the computer.
Rex, der Dinosaurier, ist oben auf meinem Computer.

computer game das Computerspiel
Max likes to play computer games on my computer.
Max spielt auf meinem Computer gern Computerspiele.

doll die Puppe
My favourite doll is called Sally.
Meine Lieblingspuppe heißt Sally.

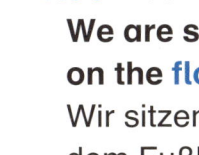

desk der Schreibtisch
I do my homework at my desk.
Ich mache meine Hausaufgaben an meinem Schreibtisch.

floor der Boden, der Fußboden
We are sitting on the floor.
Wir sitzen auf dem Fußboden.

dice die Würfel
Throw the dice.
Würfle.

game das Spiel
I'm playing a game with Holly and Jake.
Ich spiele mit Holly und Jake ein Spiel.

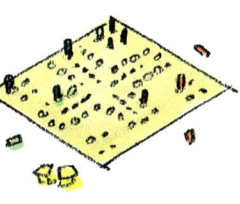

My room, my toys

keyboard die Tastatur
The computer keyboard is on the desk.
Die Computertastatur ist auf dem Schreibtisch.

lamp die Lampe
What colour is my lamp?
Welche Farbe hat meine Lampe?

mobile phone das Handy
Where is my mobile phone?
Wo ist mein Handy?

mouse pad das Mauspad
The mouse is on the mouse pad.
Die Maus ist auf dem Mauspad.

piggy bank das Sparschwein
My piggy bank isn't very heavy.
Mein Sparschwein ist nicht sehr schwer.

pillow das Kopfkissen
Aah, my pillow is lovely and soft.
Ah, mein Kopfkissen ist schön weich.

poster das Poster
Can you see the poster of my favourite pop group?
Siehst du das Poster von meiner Lieblingsgruppe?

radio das Radio
I sometimes listen to the radio in the morning.
Manchmal höre ich morgens Radio.

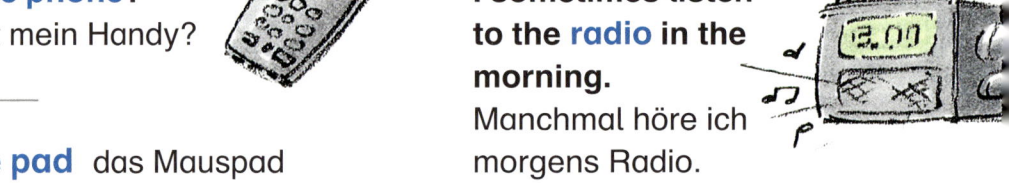

roller-blades die Inliner
Where are my roller-blades?
Wo sind meine Inliner?

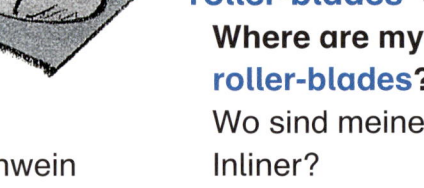

room das Zimmer
This is my room, and I love it.
Dies ist mein Zimmer, und ich liebe es.

My room, my toys

shelf das Regal
There are lots of books on the shelf.
Auf dem Regal sind viele Bücher.

tennis ball der Tennisball
What colour are the tennis balls?
Welche Farbe haben die Tennisbälle?

to sit sitzen
Queenie is sitting in her basket.
Queenie sitzt in ihrem Körbchen.

tennis racket der Tennisschläger
My tennis racket is very old.
Mein Tennisschläger ist sehr alt.

sometimes manchmal
Queenie sometimes sleeps on my bed.
Manchmal schläft Queenie auf meinem Bett.

toy das Spielzeug
The boxes are full of toys.
Die Schachteln sind voll mit Spielzeug.

teddy bear der Teddybär
My teddy bear always sleeps on my bed.
Mein Teddybär schläft immer auf meinem Bett.

wall die Wand
The poster is on the wall above my bed.
Das Poster ist an der Wand über meinem Bett.

window das Fenster
My desk is in front of the window.
Mein Schreibtisch steht vor dem Fenster.

My body

nose

mouth

foot

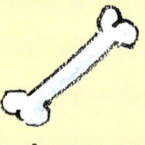
bone

doctor

eye

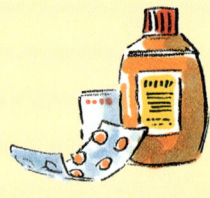
ear

medicine

elbow

arm

plaster

mirror

leg

bandage

thumb

toe

knee

My body

arm der Arm
  **Max's arms are
  very muddy.**
  Max' Arme sind
  sehr dreckig.

back der Rücken
  Mum's back hurts.
  Mamas Rücken
  tut weh.

bandage der Verband
  **Teddy has a bandage
  around his head.**
  Teddy hat einen
  Verband um den Kopf.

to bleed bluten
  **Max's knee is
  bleeding.**
  Max' Knie blutet.

blonde blond
  I have blonde hair.
  Ich habe blondes Haar.

body der Körper
  My body hurts.
  Mein Körper tut weh.

bone der Knochen
  **Mia has hurt her toe
  on Queenie's bone.**
  Mia hat ihren Zeh
  an Queenies Knochen
  gestoßen.

bottom der Po, der Hintern
  **The baby has
  fallen down and
  hurt his bottom.**
  Das Baby ist hin-
  gefallen und hat sich
  am Po wehgetan.

bruise der blaue Fleck
  **Mia has a bruise
  on her leg.**
  Mia hat einen blauen
  Fleck am Bein.

to bump anstoßen
  **Mia has bumped
  her toe.**
  Mia hat sich den
  Zeh angestoßen.

My body

chest die Brust
The doctor is listening to my chest.
Die Ärztin hört meine Brust ab.

dirty schmutzig
Why is Max so dirty?
Warum ist Max so schmutzig?

chin das Kinn
Dad has a plaster on his chin.
Papa hat ein Pflaster am Kinn.

doctor der Arzt, die Ärztin
The doctor is a very nice lady.
Die Ärztin ist eine sehr nette Frau.

cold die Erkältung
I think I have a cold.
Ich glaube, ich habe eine Erkältung.

ear das Ohr
Queenie is scratching her ear.
Queenie kratzt sich am Ohr.

cough der Husten
The doctor gave me medicine for my cough.
Die Ärztin gab mir Medizin für meinen Husten.

earache die Ohrenschmerzen
My ears hurt. I have horrible earache.
Meine Ohren tun weh. Ich habe schreckliche Ohrenschmerzen.

curly lockig
Do you have curly hair?
Hast du lockiges Haar?

elbow der Ellenbogen
Max bumped his elbow.
Max hat sich am Ellenbogen gestoßen.

My body

eye das Auge
The bandage is over Teddy's eye.
Der Verband ist über Teddys Auge.

eyebrow die Augenbraue
Your eyebrows are above your eyes.
Die Augenbrauen sind über deinen Augen.

face das Gesicht
Max has a very dirty face.
Max hat ein sehr schmutziges Gesicht.

to fall down hinfallen
Max fell down when he was playing football.
Max ist beim Fußballspielen hingefallen.

to feel fühlen
I feel ill.
Ich fühle mich krank.

feet die Füße
My feet are cold.
Meine Füße sind kalt.

finger der Finger
How many fingers do you have?
Wie viele Finger hast du?

foot der Fuß
The baby can put his foot into his mouth.
Das Baby kann seinen Fuß in den Mund nehmen.

hair das Haar
Grandma has grey hair.
Oma hat graues Haar.

hand die Hand
The baby's hands are very small. Uncle Bill's hands are very big.
Babys Hände sind sehr klein. Onkel Bills Hände sind sehr groß.

My body

to have a bath ein Bad nehmen
Max needs to have a bath.
Max muss ein Bad nehmen.

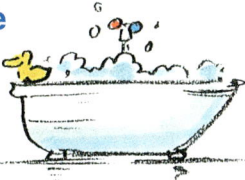

___

head der Kopf
My head is hot.
Mein Kopf ist heiß.

___

headache die Kopfschmerzen
Our teacher sometimes has a headache.
Unsere Lehrerin hat manchmal Kopfschmerzen.

___

to hear hören
Can you hear the rain?
Kannst du den Regen hören?

___

to hurt wehtun
My head hurts.
Mein Kopf tut weh.

ill krank
I feel ill.
Ich fühle mich krank.

___

knee das Knie
Max has hurt his knee.
Max hat sich am Knie wehgetan.

___

leg das Bein
I have two legs. Queenie has four legs.
Ich habe zwei Beine. Queenie hat vier Beine.

___

to look aussehen
Max looks dirty.
Max sieht schmutzig aus.

___

medicine
die Medizin, das Medikament
The doctor has lots of medicine in her bag.
Die Ärztin hat eine Menge Medikamente in ihrer Tasche.

My body

mirror der Spiegel
What can Max see in the mirror?
Was kann Max im Spiegel sehen?

moustache der Schnurrbart
Does your dad have a moustache?
Hat dein Papa einen Schnurrbart?

mouth der Mund
The baby can put his foot into his mouth.
Das Baby kann seinen Fuß in den Mund nehmen.

neck der Hals
Giraffes have very, very long necks.
Giraffen haben einen sehr sehr langen Hals.

nose die Nase
I have a red nose.
Ich habe eine rote Nase.

ouch! autsch!
Ouch! Mia has hurt her toe.
Autsch! Mia hat sich am Zeh wehgetan.

plaster das Pflaster
Max has a plaster on his knee.
Max hat ein Pflaster am Knie.

to scratch kratzen
Queenie is scratching her ear.
Queenie kratzt sich am Ohr.

to see sehen
Mia didn't see Queenie's bone.
Mia hat Queenies Knochen nicht gesehen.

shoulder die Schulter
Winston is sitting on Aunt Lizzie's shoulder.
Winston sitzt auf Tante Lizzies Schulter.

My body

to sneeze niesen
I have to sneeze a lot today. Aatchoo!
Ich muss heute viel niesen. Hatschi!

toe der Zeh
How many toes do you have?
Wie viele Zehen hast du?

sore throat die Halsschmerzen
I have a sore throat.
Ich habe Halsschmerzen.

toothache die Zahnschmerzen
Brush your teeth every day, then you won't have toothache.
Putz deine Zähne jeden Tag, dann bekommst du keine Zahnschmerzen.

straight glatt, gerade
Rita has very straight hair.
Rita hat sehr glatte Haare.

tummy der Bauch
Queenie likes having her tummy scratched.
Queenie lässt sich gern am Bauch kratzen.

to talk sprechen
I can't talk today.
Ich kann heute nicht sprechen.

to wash sich waschen

Go and have a wash!
Geh und wasch dich!

thumb der Daumen
The baby sleeps with his thumb in his mouth.
Das Baby schläft mit dem Daumen im Mund.

Feelings

cry

sad

sleeping bag

tent

to laugh

pancake

smile

love

dentist

hide

Feelings

to agree zustimmen
I agree with you.
Ich stimme dir zu.

angry wütend
Lady Slow is angry because Buttercup has eaten her lunch.
Lady Slow ist wütend, weil Buttercup ihr Mittagessen aufgefressen hat.

to be afraid of Angst haben vor
The mouse is not afraid of the cat.
Die Maus hat keine Angst vor der Katze.

beautiful schön
Buttercup has beautiful, big, black eyes.
Buttercup hat schöne, große, schwarze Augen.

to believe glauben
Do you believe in monsters?
Glaubst du an Monster?

to be scared of Angst haben vor
I'm scared of the dentist.
Ich habe Angst vor dem Zahnarzt.

to be sorry Leid tun
Oh, I'm very sorry.
Oh, es tut mir sehr Leid.

better besser
I feel better now.
Mir geht's jetzt besser.

bicycle das Fahrrad
Mum loves riding her bicycle.
Mama liebt es, mit dem Fahrrad zu fahren.

bike das Fahrrad
Mia has a shiny red bike.
Mia hat ein glänzendes rotes Fahrrad.

Feelings

boring langweilig
Playing hide and seek with Lady Slow is really boring.
Mit Lady Slow Verstecken zu spielen ist sehr langweilig.

excellent hervorragend, ausgezeichnet
Grandma makes excellent pancakes.
Oma macht ausgezeichnete Pfannkuchen.

clever schlau, klug
My dog, Queenie, is very clever.
Mein Hund, Queenie, ist sehr schlau.

famous berühmt
Papa flies famous people around the world.
Berühmte Leute fliegen mit Papa um die Welt.

to cry weinen
The baby is crying.
Das Baby weint.

friendly freundlich
Mum says that the dentist is friendly.
Mama sagt, dass der Zahnarzt freundlich ist.

dentist der Zahnarzt, die Zahnärztin
I don't like the dentist.
Ich mag den Zahnarzt nicht.

fun der Spaß
It's fun to sleep in a tent.
Es macht Spaß, in einem Zelt zu schlafen.

early früh
I don't want to get up so early.
Ich will nicht so früh aufstehen.

happy glücklich
Buttercup is happy.
Buttercup ist glücklich.

Feelings

to hate hassen
Mum hates washing the dishes.
Mama hasst abspülen.

helicopter der Hubschrauber
Dad's friend is a helicopter pilot.
Papas Freund ist Hubschrauberpilot.

to hide verstecken
Lady Slow is hiding.
Lady Slow versteckt sich.

hide and seek Verstecken
It's no fun playing hide and seek with a tortoise.
Es macht keinen Spaß, mit einer Schildkröte Verstecken zu spielen.

horrible schrecklich, grauenhaft
The baby thinks vegetables taste horrible.
Das Baby findet, dass Gemüse grauenhaft schmeckt.

to hug umarmen
I'm hugging Queenie.
Ich umarme Queenie.

hungry hungrig
Queenie is very hungry.
Queenie ist sehr hungrig.

interesting interessant
Max thinks spiders are very interesting.
Max findet Spinnen sehr interessant.

joke der Witz
Max is telling Dad a joke.
Max erzählt Papa einen Witz.

late spät
It's very late. Mia is tired.
Es ist sehr spät. Mia ist müde.

Feelings

to laugh lachen
  Dad is laughing at Max's joke.
  Papa lacht über Max' Witz.

noisy laut
  The helicopter is very noisy.
  Der Hubschrauber ist sehr laut.

library die Bücherei, die Bibliothek
  Mum likes going to the library.
  Mama geht gern zur Bücherei.

to not feel well sich unwohl fühlen
  Max doesn't feel well.
  Max fühlt sich unwohl.

to like mögen
  Do you like pancakes?
  Magst du Pfannkuchen?

nothing nichts
  There's nothing in the box.
  In der Schachtel ist nichts.

to love lieben
  Max loves pancakes.
  Max liebt Pfannkuchen.

pancake der Pfannkuchen
  Max has eaten fifteen pancakes.
  Max hat fünfzehn Pfannkuchen gegessen.

lovely schön
  What a lovely day, thinks Buttercup.
  Was für ein schöner Tag, denkt Buttercup.

sad traurig
  The baby is sad because Winston doesn't want to play with him.
  Das Baby ist traurig, weil Winston nicht mit ihm spielen will.

Feelings

sleeping bag der Schlafsack
Max and Mia like sleeping in sleeping bags.
Max und Mia schlafen gern im Schlafsack.

to smell riechen
Don't the roses smell lovely?
Riechen die Rosen nicht gut?

smell der Geruch
What's that horrible smell?
Was ist das für ein schrecklicher Geruch?

to smile lächeln
Aunt Lizzie is smiling at the baby. Winston is not smiling.
Tante Lizzie lächelt das Baby an. Winston lächelt nicht.

something etwas
Winston thinks there is something hiding in the box.
Winston glaubt, dass etwas in der Schachtel versteckt ist.

to taste schmecken
Buttercup thinks that Lady Slow's lunch tastes lovely.
Buttercup findet, dass Lady Slows Mittagessen prima schmeckt.

to tell erzählen
Tell me a joke.
Erzähl mir einen Witz.

tent das Zelt
It's no fun sleeping in a tent in the rain.
Es macht keinen Spaß, bei Regen in einem Zelt zu schlafen.

Feelings

thing das Ding
I don't like that thing.
Das Ding mag ich nicht.

thirsty durstig
We are thirsty after our long walk.
Wir sind durstig nach unserem langen Spaziergang.

tired müde
Mia is tired. She wants to go to sleep.
Mia ist müde. Sie will schlafen.

too many zu viel
Max has eaten too many pancakes.
Max hat zu viele Pfannkuchen gegessen.

very much sehr
The baby likes Winston very much.
Das Baby mag Winston sehr.

to want wollen
The baby wants to play with Winston.
Das Baby will mit Winston spielen.

to wash the dishes abspülen
Someone must wash the dishes.
Jemand muss das Geschirr abspülen.

Clothes

sock

wardrobe

gloves

trainers

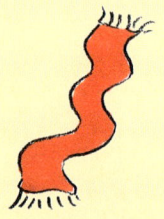
scarf

jumper

boots

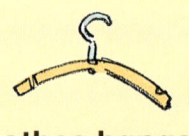
clothes hanger

tie

watch

pyjamas

trousers

button

slipper

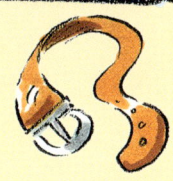
necklace

belt

shoe

45

Clothes

bag die Tasche
Where is my bag?
Wo ist meine Tasche?

baseball der Baseball
Max puts on his cap when he plays baseball.
Max setzt beim Baseballspielen seine Mütze auf.

belt der Gürtel
My belt holds up my trousers.
Mein Gürtel hält meine Hose.

blanket die Decke
Queenie has a blanket in her bed.
Queenie hat eine Decke in ihrem Bett.

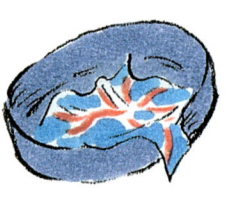

blouse die Bluse
I always wear a white blouse to school.
Ich trage immer eine weiße Bluse zur Schule.

boots die Stiefel
I like to wear boots in the rain.
Bei Regen trage ich gerne Stiefel.

bracelet das Armband
Grandma gave me this bracelet for my birthday.
Oma hat mir dieses Armband zum meinem Geburtstag geschenkt.

to bring bringen
Queenie, bring me my slipper!
Queenie, bring mir meinen Hausschuh!

button der Knopf
How many gold buttons are on my coat?
Wie viele goldene Knöpfe sind an meinem Mantel?

cap die Mütze
Max has his baseball cap on his head.
Max hat seine Baseballmütze auf dem Kopf.

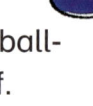

Clothes

clothes die Kleidung
I have lots of clothes.
Ich habe viele Kleidungsstücke.

dressing gown der Bademantel, der Morgenmantel
My dressing gown is lovely and warm.
Mein Morgenmantel ist kuschelig warm.

clothes hanger der Kleiderbügel
My winter coat is hanging on a clothes hanger.
Mein Wintermantel hängt auf einem Kleiderbügel.

everywhere überall
My clothes are everywhere.
Meine Kleider sind überall.

gloves die Handschuhe
Gloves keep my hands warm in winter.
In Winter halten Handschuhe meine Hände warm.

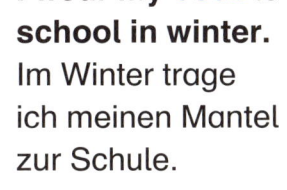

coat der Mantel
I wear my coat to school in winter.
Im Winter trage ich meinen Mantel zur Schule.

to hang hängen
My jacket is hanging on the wardrobe door.
Meine Jacke hängt an der Kleiderschranktür.

dress das Kleid
Grandma has lots of lovely dresses.
Oma hat viele schöne Kleider.

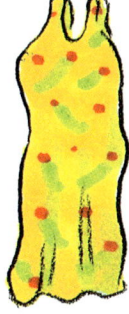

Clothes

hat der Hut
Mum's hat keeps the sun out of her eyes.
Mamas Hut schützt ihre Augen vor der Sonne.

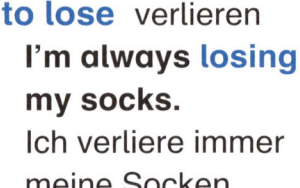

hole das Loch
There's a hole in my sock. I can see my toe.
In meiner Socke ist ein Loch. Ich kann meinen Zeh sehen.

jacket die Jacke
Queenie is wearing her favourite jacket.
Queenie trägt ihre Lieblingsjacke.

jeans die Jeans
Mia is wearing jeans today.
Heute trägt Mia ihre Jeans.

jumper der Pullover
Grandma made Mia's jumper.
Oma hat Mias Pullover gestrickt.

to lose verlieren
I'm always losing my socks.
Ich verliere immer meine Socken.

mess die Unordnung
My room is in a mess.
In meinem Zimmer herrscht Unordnung.

necklace die Halskette
Grandma gave me this necklace, too.
Oma hat mir auch diese Halskette geschenkt.

pair das Paar
Why can't I find a pair of socks?
Warum kann ich kein Paar Socken finden?

pocket die Hosentasche
What is in Max's pocket?
Was ist in Max' Hosentasche?

Clothes

problem das Problem
**I've got a problem.
I can't find my sock.**
Ich habe ein Problem.
Ich kann meine Socke
nicht finden.

pyjamas der Schlafanzug
**I wear my pyjamas
in bed.**
Im Bett trage ich einen
Schlafanzug.

rucksack der Rucksack
**I sometimes take my
rucksack to school.**
Manchmal nehme ich
meinen Rucksack mit
in die Schule.

sandal die Sandale
**It's nice to wear
sandals in the summer.**
Es ist schön, im Sommer
Sandalen zu tragen.

scarf der Schal
**My long scarf keeps
my neck warm in winter.**
Im Winter hält mein
langer Schal meinen
Hals warm.

shall soll
**What shall I
wear today?**
Was soll ich heute
anziehen?

shirt das Hemd
**Dad has a shirt
under his jacket.**
Papa trägt ein Hemd
unter seinem Jackett.

shoe der Schuh
**Our shoes are
downstairs in
the hall.**
Unsere Schuhe
sind unten im Flur.

shorts die Shorts, kurze Hose
**There's mud on
Max's shorts.**
Max' kurze Hosen
sind schmutzig.

Clothes

skirt der Rock
I don't like my school skirt.
Ich mag meinen Schulrock nicht.

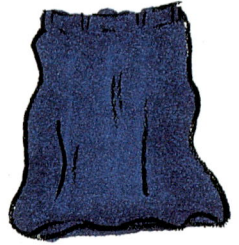

slipper der Hausschuh
Queenie loves my slippers.
Queenie liebt meine Hausschuhe.

sock die Socke
Where's my sock?
Wo ist meine Socke?

to steal stehlen
Who stole my slippers?
Wer hat meine Hausschuhe gestohlen?

stripy gestreift
Where is my stripy sock?
Wo ist meine gestreifte Socke?

to tidy up aufräumen
Penny, please tidy up your room.
Penny, bitte räum dein Zimmer auf.

tie die Krawatte
Do you like Dad's tie?
Magst du Papas Krawatte?

tights die Strumpfhose
I wear tights under my skirt.
Ich trage Strumpfhosen unter meinem Rock.

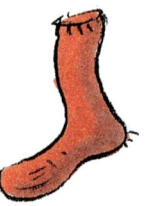

trainers die Turnschuhe
Max can run very fast in his new trainers.
In seinen neuen Turnschuhen kann Max sehr schnell laufen.

Clothes

trousers die Hose
Max's school trousers are always dirty.
Max' Schulhosen sind immer schmutzig.

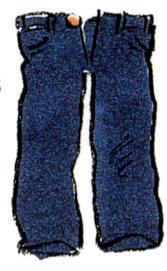

to try on anprobieren
Mum and I like to try on new hats.
Mama und ich probieren gern neue Hüte an.

T-shirt das T-Shirt
We wear T-shirts when we do sports.
Beim Sport tragen wir T-Shirts.

underwear die Unterwäsche
I'm cold in my underwear.
Mir ist kalt in meiner Unterwäsche.

wardrobe der Kleiderschrank
There are lots of clothes in my wardrobe.
Es sind viele Kleidungsstücke in meinem Schrank.

watch die Armbanduhr
Mia got a new watch for her birthday.
Mia hat eine neue Armbanduhr zu ihrem Geburtstag bekommen.

to wear tragen
I don't know what to wear today.
Ich weiß nicht, was ich heute anziehen soll.

My day

clock

teeth

king

moon

queen

star

to sleep

to get up

dinner

crown   toast   toothbrush   toothpaste

My day

after nach
- **I do my homework after school.**
- Nach der Schule mache ich meine Hausaufgaben.

---

afternoon der Nachmittag
- **In England we always have school in the afternoons.**
- In England haben wir immer nachmittags Schule.

---

always immer
- **I always read in bed.**
- Ich lese immer im Bett.

---

before vor
- **I usually do my homework before dinner.**
- Normalerweise mache ich meine Hausaufgaben vor dem Abendessen.

to begin anfangen
- **We begin school at quarter to nine.**
- Bei uns fängt die Schule um Viertel vor neun an.

---

breakfast das Frühstück
- **Queenie always eats her breakfast under the kitchen table.**
- Queenie isst ihr Frühstück immer unter dem Tisch.

---

to brush one's teeth sich die Zähne putzen
- **Don't forget to brush your teeth after breakfast.**
- Vergiss nicht, deine Zähne nach dem Frühstück zu putzen.

---

bye tschüs
- **Bye.**
- Tschüs.

My day

clock die Uhr
The clock in the hall is broken.
Die Uhr im Flur ist kaputt.

---

to come kommen
Dad is coming home from work.
Papa kommt gerade von der Arbeit zurück.

---

crown die Krone
Can you see the golden crown?
Siehst du die goldene Krone?

---

dark dunkel
In winter it's dark at five o'clock in the afternoon.
Im Winter ist es um fünf Uhr nachmittags dunkel.

---

day der Tag
Saturday is my favourite day of the week.
Samstag ist mein Lieblingstag.

---

dinner das Abendessen
We have dinner at six o'clock in the evening.
Das Abendessen gibt es bei uns um sechs Uhr abends.

---

to do machen
I don't like doing my homework.
Ich mache nicht gerne Hausaufgaben.

---

evening der Abend
There's a good film on TV this evening.
Heute Abend kommt ein toller Film im Fernsehen.

---

to get up aufstehen
I get up at seven thirty in the morning.
Ich stehe morgens um sieben Uhr dreißig auf.

My day

goodbye auf Wiedersehen

Goodbye.
Auf Wiedersehen.

good morning guten Morgen

Good morning.
Guten Morgen.

good night gute Nacht

Good night.
Gute Nacht.

to have breakfast frühstücken
We have breakfast at the kitchen table.
Wir frühstücken am Küchentisch.

to have a shower duschen
I sometimes have a shower in the evening.
Manchmal dusche ich abends.

homework die Hausaufgaben
Mum sometimes helps me with my homework.
Mama hilft mir manchmal bei den Hausaufgaben.

hour die Stunde
There are twenty-four hours in a day.
Ein Tag hat 24 Stunden.

king der König
I'm reading a book about a king and a queen.
Ich lese ein Buch über einen König und eine Königin.

My day

lunch das Mittagessen
I take sandwiches to school for lunch.
Ich nehme mir Sandwichs zum Mittagessen in die Schule mit.

moon der Mond
Queenie always barks at the full moon.
Queenie bellt immer den Vollmond an.

lunch break die Mittagspause
We go out into the playground in the lunch break.
In der Mittagspause gehen wir raus auf den Schulhof.

morning der Morgen, der Vormittag
We have a fifteen minute break at school in the morning.
Wir haben eine fünfzehnminütige Pause morgens in der Schule.

midnight Mitternacht
Ghosts come out to play at midnight.
Gespenster kommen um Mitternacht zum Spielen heraus.

night die Nacht
Bats and owls fly at night.
Fledermäuse und Eulen fliegen in der Nacht.

minute die Minute
There are sixty minutes in an hour.
Eine Stunde hat 60 Minuten.

queen die Königin
In my book, the queen has lost her crown.
In meinem Buch hat die Königin ihre Krone verloren.

57

My day

star der Stern
How many stars can you see?
Wie viele Sterne kannst du sehen?

toast der Toast
Today I'm having toast for breakfast.
Heute esse ich Toast zum Frühstück.

time die Zeit
What time do you begin school?
Zu welcher Zeit fängt bei dir die Schule an?

tonight heute Abend
There's a full moon tonight.
Heute Abend ist Vollmond.

tired müde
Mum is very tired this morning.
Mama ist heute Morgen sehr müde.

tooth der Zahn
The baby has one tooth.
Das Baby hat einen Zahn.

to sleep schlafen
Max watched a monster film. Now he can't sleep.
Max schaute einen Gruselfilm an. Jetzt kann er nicht schlafen.

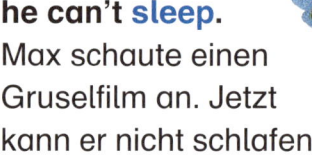

toothbrush die Zahnbürste
What colour is your toothbrush?
Welche Farbe hat deine Zahnbürste?

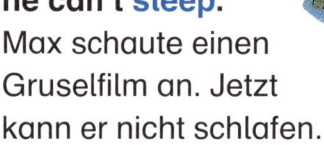

toothpaste die Zahnpasta
Where's the toothpaste?
Wo ist die Zahnpasta?

teeth die Zähne
Grandpa has no teeth.
Opa hat keine Zähne.

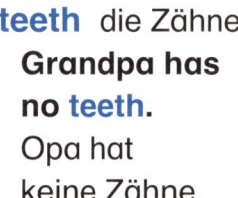

My day

usually gewöhnlich, normalerweise
I usually drink a cup of tea in the morning.
Normalerweise trinke ich morgens eine Tasse Tee.

---

to wake up aufwecken
Queenie always wakes me up at the weekend.
Am Wochenende weckt mich Queenie immer auf.

---

walk der Spaziergang
I always go for a walk with Queenie in the afternoon.
Nachmittags gehe ich immer mit Queenie spazieren.

to walk zu Fuß gehen
I usually walk to school.
Ich gehe gewöhnlich zu Fuß zur Schule.

---

to watch tv fernsehen
We like to watch tv after dinner.
Nach dem Abendessen sehen wir gerne fern.

---

with mit
I walk to school with Holly and Jake.
Ich gehe mit Holly und Jake zur Schule.

Time	Uhrzeit
What's the time?	Wie viel Uhr ist es?
It's 9 o'clock	Es ist 9 Uhr.
half an hour	halbe Stunde
half past nine	halb zehn
quarter past nine	Viertel nach neun
quarter to nine	Viertel vor neun

At school

book

bell

paintbrush

pencil sharpener

felt tip pen

glue

pencil case

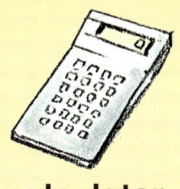 

calculator **pen**

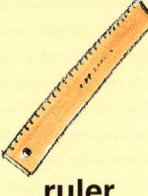

scissors

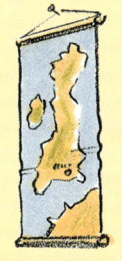

ruler

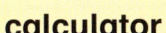

map

cage

hamster **globe** **dictionary** **pencil**

61

At school

alphabet das Alphabet
The alphabet begins with A.
Das Alphabet fängt mit A an.

---

answer die Antwort
Rita knows the answer.
Rita weiß die Antwort.

art Kunst
We have art this afternoon.
Heute Nachmittag haben wir Kunst.

---

to ask fragen
Ask me a question.
Frag mich was.

---

bell die Glocke
The bell is next to the clock.
Die Glocke ist neben der Uhr.

blackboard die Tafel
Mrs Wise is writing on the blackboard with chalk.
Frau Wise schreibt mit Kreide an die Tafel.

---

book das Buch
The children's books are on their desks.
Die Bücher der Kinder sind auf ihren Schreibtischen.

---

bookcase das Bücherregal
There are lots of books in the bookcase.
Im Bücherregal sind eine Menge Bücher.

---

break die Pause
We have a fifteen minute break in the morning.
Wir haben morgens eine fünfzehnminütige Pause.

At school

cage der Käfig
  **Furball's cage is
  next to the window.**
  Furballs Käfig steht
  neben dem Fenster.

calculator der Taschenrechner
  **Jake has a calculator
  in his bag.**
  Jake hat einen
  Taschenrechner
  in seiner Tasche.

can können
  **Can I have your
  ruler, please?
  Yes, you can.**
  Kann ich bitte dein
  Lineal haben? Ja.

chalk die Kreide
  The chalk is white.
  Die Kreide ist weiß.

classroom das Klassenzimmer
  **This is my
  classroom.**
  Dies ist mein
  Klassenzimmer.

to cut schneiden
  **It's easy to cut paper
  with scissors.**
  Es ist einfach, Papier
  mit einer Schere zu
  schneiden.

dictionary das Lexikon,
das Wörterbuch
  **Do you have
  a dictionary?**
  Hast du ein
  Wörterbuch?

favourite Lieblings-
  **My favourite lesson
  is art.**
  Meine Lieblingsstunde
  ist Kunst.

felt tip pen der Filzstift
  **Rita has lots of
  felt tip pens.**
  Rita hat viele
  Filzstifte.

French Französisch
  **In England we learn
  French at school.**
  In England lernen wir
  Französisch in der Schule.

At school

Geography Erdkunde
I like our Geography lessons too.
Ich mag auch unsere Erdkundestunden.

globe der Globus
I can see the USA on the globe.
Auf dem Globus kann ich die USA sehen.

glue der Klebstoff
The glue is next to the scissors.
Der Klebstoff ist neben der Schere.

Great Britain Großbritannien
Can you see Great Britain on the map?
Kannst du Großbritannien auf der Karte sehen?

to guess erraten
Can you guess the answer?
Kannst du die Antwort erraten?

hamster der Hamster
The school hamster is called Furball.
Der Schulhamster heißt Furball.

help helfen
Can you help me, please?
Kannst du mir bitte helfen?

History Geschichte
We are learning about Kings and Queens in History.
In Geschichte lernen wir etwas über Könige und Königinnen.

to know wissen, kennen
Rita knows the answer.
Rita weiß die Antwort.

At school

language die Sprache
How many languages can you speak?
Wie viele Sprachen sprichst du?

to learn lernen
Do you learn English at school?
Lernst du Englisch in der Schule?

lesson die Unterrichtsstunde
Jake's favourite lesson is Sport.
Jakes Lieblingsstunde ist Sport.

letter der Buchstabe
A is the first letter of the alphabet.
A ist der erste Buchstabe des Alphabets.

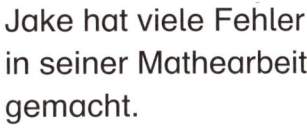

to make machen
Rita didn't make any mistakes in her maths test.
Rita hat keine Fehler in ihrer Mathearbeit gemacht.

map die Landkarte
The map is on the wall between the windows.
Die Landkarte hängt an der Wand zwischen den Fenstern.

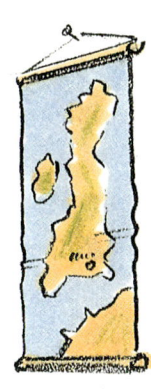

maths Mathematik
I don't like maths.
Ich mag Mathematik nicht.

$2+2=5$

mistake der Fehler
Jake made a lot of mistakes in his maths test.
Jake hat viele Fehler in seiner Mathearbeit gemacht.

page die Seite
What page are we on?
Auf welcher Seite sind wir?

to paint malen
We do lots of painting in the art lesson.
Wir malen viel in der Kunststunde.

At school

paintbrush der Pinsel
The paintbrushes are next to Furball's cage.
Die Pinsel sind neben Furballs Käfig.

paper das Papier
We need lots of paper at school.
In der Schule brauchen wir viel Papier.

pen der Stift
Holly is writing with her pen in her book.
Holly schreibt mit einem Stift in ihr Buch.

pencil der Bleistift
The pencil is under the desk.
Der Bleistift ist unter dem Schreibtisch.

pencil case das Mäppchen
Rita has lots of pencils in her pencil case.
Rita hat viele Stifte in ihrem Mäppchen.

pencil sharpener der Bleistiftspitzer
My pencil's broken. Do you have a pencil sharpener?
Mein Bleistift ist abgebrochen. Hast du einen Spitzer?

pupil der Schüler, die Schülerin
How many pupils are in your class?
Wie viele Schüler sind in deiner Klasse?

question die Frage
Jake is asking Penny a question.
Jake stellt Penny eine Frage.

to ring klingeln
The bell rings when it's time for lunch.
Wenn es Zeit fürs Mittagessen ist, klingelt die Glocke.

At school

rubber (BE) der Radiergummi
Where is my rubber?
Wo ist mein Radier-gummi?

ruler das Lineal
Can I have your ruler, please?
Kann ich bitte dein Lineal haben?

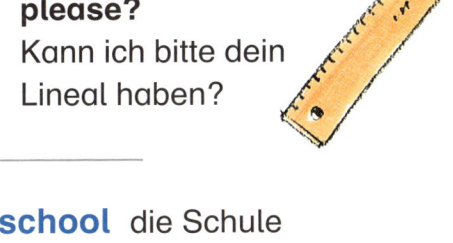

school die Schule
In England children start school when they are five years old.
In England kommen die Kinder mit fünf Jahren in die Schule.

school playground der Schulhof
Sanjay is in the school playground.
Sanjay ist auf dem Schulhof.

scissors die Schere
Where are the scissors?
Wo ist die Schere?

to sit down sich hinsetzen
Sit down, please.
Setz dich, bitte.

subject das Fach
What's your favourite school subject?
Was ist dein Lieblingsfach?

to take nehmen
You can't take your dog to school.
Du kannst deinen Hund nicht mit zur Schule nehmen.

to teach unterrichten
Mrs Wise is teaching us maths.
Frau Wise unterrichtet Mathe.

teacher der Lehrer, die Lehrerin
Our teacher is called Mrs Wise.
Unsere Lehrerin heißt Frau Wise.

At school

test eine Klassenarbeit
Yesterday we had an English test.
Gestern haben wir eine Englischarbeit geschrieben.

---

tick der Haken
The teacher puts a tick next to the right answers.
Die Lehrerin macht einen Haken neben die richtigen Antworten.

---

timetable der Stundenplan
The timetable for today is on the wall.
Der Stundenplan für heute hängt an der Wand.

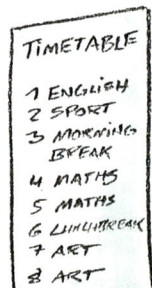

---

to use benutzen
We use the paints in the art lesson.
Wir benutzen die Farben in Kunst.

to wave winken
Can you see Sanjay waving?
Kannst du Sanjay winken sehen?

---

to whisper flüstern
Jake is whispering to me.
Jake flüstert mir zu.

---

world die Welt
You can see the world on the globe.
Du kannst die Welt auf dem Globus sehen.

---

words die Wörter
How many words are there in the dictionary?
Wie viele Wörter sind in dem Wörterbuch?

---

to write schreiben
The teacher is writing on the blackboard.
Die Lehrerin schreibt an die Tafel.

At school

Classroom Phrases	Was ihr im Klassenzimmer hört
Can I have your ruler, please?	Kann ich bitte dein Lineal haben?
I don't understand the question.	Ich verstehe die Frage nicht.
Can you say that again, please?	Können Sie das bitte noch mal sagen?
Stand up, please.	Bitte aufstehen.
Sit down, please.	Bitte hinsetzen.
Open your books at page 12.	Öffnet eure Bücher auf Seite 12.
Shut your books, please.	Bitte macht eure Bücher zu.
Pick up your pens.	Hebt eure Stifte auf.
Close the door, please.	Bitte macht die Tür zu.
Be quiet, please.	Seid bitte leise.
Write the answers in your book.	Schreibt die Antworten in euer Heft.

Hobbies and sports

goal

to ride a bike

goal keeper

tennis player

giant

guitar

dragon

to skip

piano

basketball

to ice skate

forest

to run   to sing   football   sword

Hobbies and sports

basketball der Basketball
Tortoises can't play basketball.
Schildkröten können nicht Basketball spielen.

busy beschäftigt
Aunt Lizzie is very busy in the kitchen.
Tante Lizzie ist in der Küche sehr beschäftigt.

to catch fangen
Hey, Mum. Catch the ball!
He, Mama. Fang den Ball!

to collect sammeln
Dad collects flags.
Papa sammelt Flaggen.

to cook kochen
Aunt Lizzie likes cooking.
Tante Lizzie kocht gern.

to dance tanzen
Grandma and Grandpa love to dance.
Oma und Opa tanzen leidenschaftlich gern.

to do the gardening im Garten arbeiten
Mum has done the gardening. Now she is tired.
Mama hat im Garten gearbeitet. Jetzt ist sie müde.

dragon der Drache
The dragon looks very angry.
Der Drache sieht sehr wütend aus.

to draw zeichnen, malen
Max and Mia are drawing in the kitchen.
Max und Mia malen in der Küche.

Hobbies and sports

to eat essen
Queenie's hobby is eating.
Queenies Hobby ist Fressen.

goal das Fußballtor
The barn door is the goal.
Das Scheunentor ist das Fußballtor.

fairy die Fee
Mia has drawn a fairy.
Mia hat eine Fee gemalt.

goal keeper der Torwart
Max is a good goal keeper.
Max ist ein guter Torwart.

football der Fußball
Football is Max's favourite sport.
Max' Lieblingssport ist Fußball.

guitar die Gitarre
Uncle Bill can play the guitar.
Onkel Bill kann Gitarre spielen.

forest der Wald
Can you see the giant in the forest?
Siehst du den Riesen im Wald?

hobby das Hobby
Do you have a hobby?
Hast du ein Hobby?

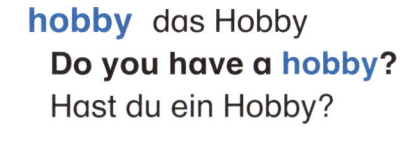

to ice skate Schlittschuh laufen
Buttercup can't ice skate.
Buttercup kann nicht Schlittschuh laufen.

giant der Riese
Max has drawn a giant in the forest.
Max hat einen Riesen im Wald gemalt.

Hobbies and sports

knight der Ritter
The knight is holding a long sword.
Der Ritter hält ein langes Schwert.

---

to like (doing something) etwas gern tun
Winston likes sleeping in front of the fire.
Winston schläft gern vor dem offenen Kamin.

---

to listen to zuhören
I like to listen to Grandma playing the piano.
Ich höre gern Oma beim Klavierspielen zu.

---

music die Musik
Do you like pop music?
Magst du Popmusik?

---

piano das Klavier
Can you play the piano?
Kannst du Klavier spielen?

to play spielen
I like playing tennis.
Ich spiele gern Tennis.

---

prince der Prinz
The prince is asleep in his castle.
Der Prinz schläft in seiner Burg.

---

princess die Prinzessin
The princess is wearing a crown.
Die Prinzessin trägt eine Krone.

---

to ride a bike Rad fahren
Mum is riding her bike to town.
Mama fährt mit dem Fahrrad in die Stadt.

---

to run laufen
Queenie is running after Mum.
Queenie läuft Mama nach.

Hobbies and sports

to sing singen
Dad always sings in the shower.
Papa singt immer unter der Dusche.

team die Mannschaft
Which is your favourite football team?
Welches ist deine Lieblingsfußballmannschaft?

to skip seilhüpfen
Mia and her friend are skipping in the school playground.
Mia und ihre Freundin hüpfen im Schulhof Seil.

tennis das Tennis
I'm playing tennis with Holly.
Ich spiele gerade mit Holly Tennis.

tennis player der Tennisspieler
Holly is not a very good tennis player.
Holly ist keine sehr gute Tennisspielerin.

story die Geschichte
Mum is reading us a story.
Mama liest uns eine Geschichte vor.

to throw werfen
Max is throwing the ball to Mum.
Max wirft Mama den Ball zu.

sword das Schwert
Max wants a sword too.
Max will auch ein Schwert haben.

to whistle pfeifen
Aunt Lizzie can whistle very loudly.
Tante Lizzie kann sehr laut pfeifen.

Food and drink

apple

cheese

orange

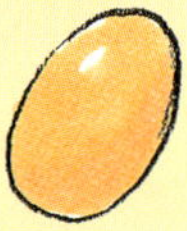

egg

 grapes

 lemon

 chocolate

 pear

crisps

banana

basket

strawberry

nut

sweet

tomato

spaghetti

77

Food and drink

apple der Apfel
Do you like green or red apples?
Magst du grüne oder rote Äpfel?

bowl die Schüssel, die Schale
Put the fruit into the fruit bowl.
Leg das Obst in die Obstschale.

banana die Banane
Where are the bananas?
Wo sind die Bananen?

butter die Butter
Put the butter in the fridge.
Leg die Butter in den Kühlschrank.

basket der Korb
What's in the basket?
Was ist in dem Korb?

to carry tragen
Mum is carrying the shopping bags.
Mama trägt die Einkaufstaschen.

bean die Bohne
Max loves beans on toast.
Max liebt Bohnen auf Toast.

cheese der Käse
Mice love cheese.
Mäuse lieben Käse.

biscuit der Keks
Grandma always eats a biscuit with her cup of tea.
Oma isst immer einen Keks zu ihrer Tasse Tee.

chocolate die Schokolade
Where has Mum hidden the chocolate?
Wo hat Mama die Schokolade versteckt?

Food and drink

coffee der Kaffee
Dad drinks lots and lots of coffee.
Papa trinkt eine Menge Kaffee.

drink das Getränk
Do you want a drink?
Willst du was zu trinken?

cream die Sahne
Winston loves cream.
Winston liebt Sahne.

to drink trinken
Grandma likes to drink tea.
Oma trinkt gerne Tee.

crisps die Chips
We sometimes take crisps to school.
Manchmal nehmen wir Chips mit in die Schule.

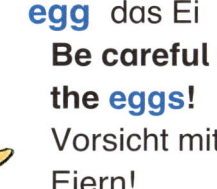

egg das Ei
Be careful with the eggs!
Vorsicht mit den Eiern!

cupboard der Schrank
Our cupboard is full of dog food.
Unser Schrank ist voll mit Hundefutter.

flour das Mehl
Grandma needs flour to bake cakes.
Oma braucht Mehl zum Kuchenbacken.

dog food Hundefutter
We need a lot of dog food.
Wir brauchen viel Hundefutter.

food die Lebensmittel
Our family eats a lot of food.
Unsere Familie verbraucht eine Menge Lebensmittel.

Food and drink

fridge der Kühlschrank
   Brrr. It's very cold inside the fridge.
   Brr. Es ist sehr kalt im Kühlschrank.

fruit das Obst
   We all eat fresh fruit every day.
   Wir essen alle jeden Tag frisches Obst.

grapes die Trauben
   What colour are the grapes?
   Welche Farbe haben die Trauben?

green pepper die grüne Paprikaschote
   I don't like green pepper.
   Ich mag keine grünen Paprika.

heavy schwer
   The shopping bags are very heavy.
   Die Einkaufstaschen sind sehr schwer.

honey der Honig
   I sometimes have honey on my toast.
   Manchmal esse ich Honig auf meinem Toast.

hot chocolate die heiße Schokolade
   We like to drink hot chocolate before we go to bed.
   Wir trinken gern heiße Schokolade, bevor wir ins Bett gehen.

jam die Marmelade
   And sometimes I have jam on my toast.
   Und manchmal esse ich Marmelade auf meinem Toast.

juice der Saft
   The twins and I like to drink apple juice.
   Die Zwillinge und ich trinken gerne Apfelsaft.

Food and drink

lemon die Zitrone
Grandma has a lemon tree.
Oma hat einen Zitronenbaum.

nice nett
Are mice nice?
Sind Mäuse nett?

melon die Melone
I always get sticky when I eat melon.
Wenn ich Melone esse, werde ich immer ganz klebrig.

nut die Nuss
The squirrels in the garden love nuts.
Die Eichhörnchen im Garten lieben Nüsse.

microwave die Mikrowelle
The microwave makes the food very hot.
Die Mikrowelle macht das Essen sehr heiß.

orange die Orange
The oranges are in the fruit bowl.
Die Orangen sind in der Obstschale.

milk die Milch
The baby likes to drink milk.
Das Baby trinkt gerne Milch.

orange juice der Orangensaft
Mum drinks orange juice in the morning.
Mama trinkt morgens Orangensaft.

muesli das Müsli
Mum always eats muesli for breakfast.
Mama ist immer Müsli zum Frühstück.

peanut butter das Erdnussbutter
Max loves peanut butter sandwiches.
Max liebt Sandwiches mit Erdnussbutter.

Food and drink

pear die Birne
The pears are in the fruit bowl, too.
Die Birnen sind auch in der Obstschale.

rice der Reis
I think rice is very nice.
Ich finde Reis sehr lecker.

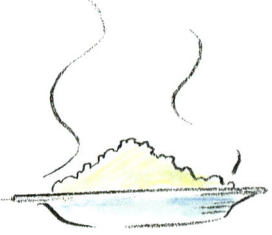

pineapple die Ananas
It's not easy to cut a pineapple.
Es ist nicht einfach, eine Ananas zu schneiden.

roll das Brötchen
I sometimes take cheese rolls to school for lunch.
Manchmal nehme ich Käsebrötchen mit zur Schule.

pizza die Pizza
My favourite food is pizza.
Pizza ist mein Lieblingsessen.

salad der Salat
Salad is good for you.
Salat ist gut für dich.

to put away wegräumen
I'm helping Mum to put away the shopping.
Ich helfe Mama gerade den Einkauf wegzuräumen.

shopping bag die Einkaufstüte
We need a lot of shopping bags for our shopping.
Wir brauchen viele Einkaufstüten für unseren Einkauf.

raspberry die Himbeere
Raspberries are Mum's favourite fruit.
Himbeeren sind Mamas Lieblingsfrüchte.

soup die Suppe
Mia likes tomato soup.
Mia mag Tomatensuppe.

Food and drink

spaghetti die Spaghetti
Eating spaghetti can be very funny.
Spaghetti essen kann sehr lustig sein.

tomato die Tomate
The tomatoes are in the fridge.
Die Tomaten sind im Kühlschrank.

strawberry die Erdbeere
I like strawberry yoghurt.
Ich mag Erdbeerjoghurt.

water das Wasser
How many bottles of water can you see?
Wie viele Flaschen Wasser kannst du sehen?

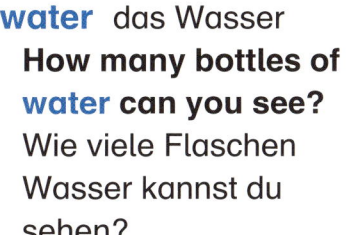

sugar der Zucker
Grandpa puts four spoons of sugar into his tea.
Opa tut vier Löffel Zucker in seinen Tee.

watermelon die Wassermelone
The big green watermelon is very heavy.
Die große grüne Wassermelone ist sehr schwer.

sweet das Bonbon
Too many sweets are bad for your teeth.
Zu viele Bonbons sind schlecht für die Zähne.

yoghurt der Joghurt
I sometimes eat yoghurt for breakfast.
Manchmal esse ich Joghurt zum Frühstück.

tea der Tee
In England people drink tea with milk.
In England trinken die Leute Tee mit Milch.

Shopping

shopping list

fish

tin

bottle

bread

purse

trolley

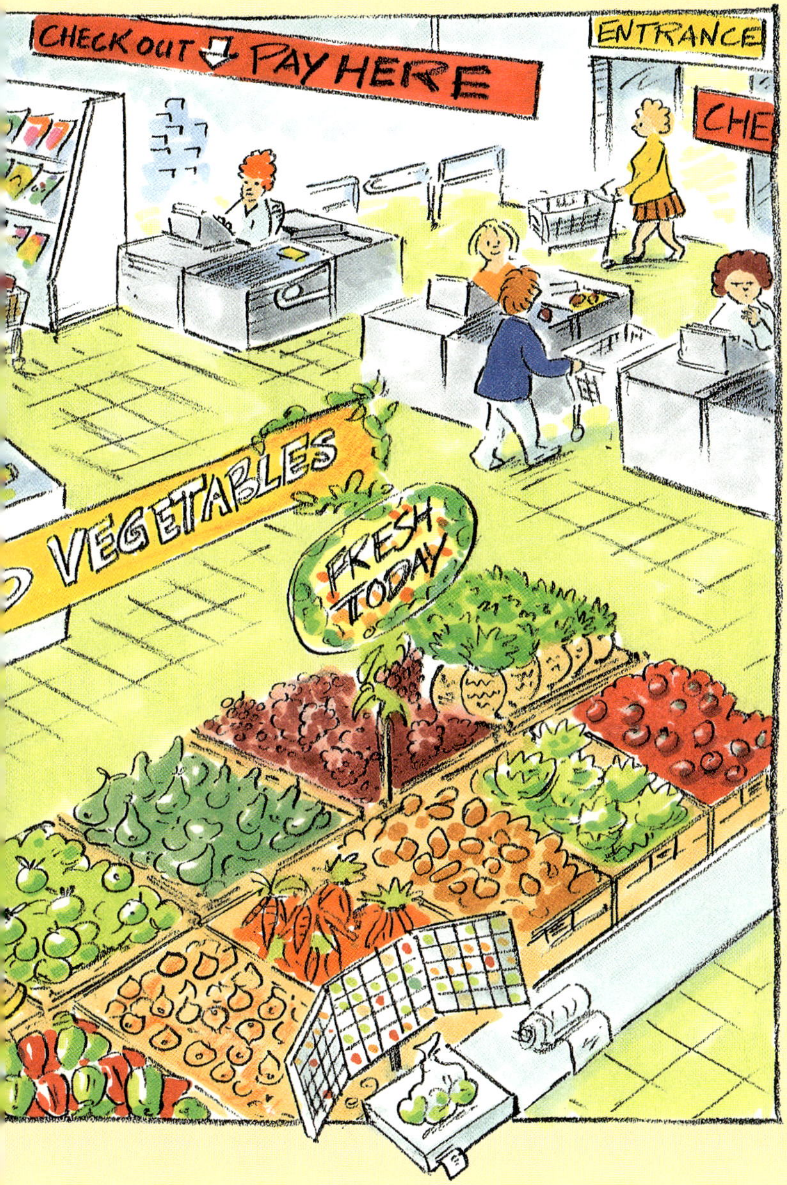

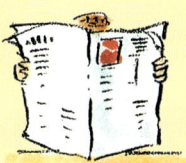

newspaper

handbag

lettuce

onion

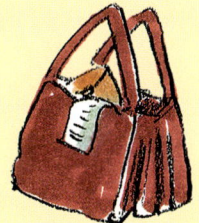

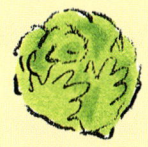

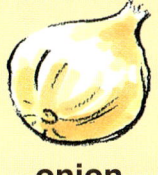

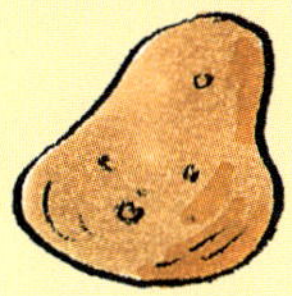

potato

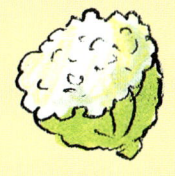

cauliflower

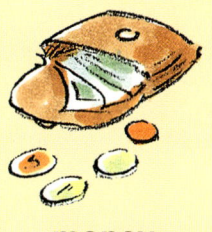

money

Shopping

bottle die Flasche
What is in the bottle?
Was ist in der Flasche?

bread das Brot
Mmm. Yummy! Fresh bread.
Mmm. Lecker! Frisches Brot.

to buy kaufen
We need to buy a lot of food.
Wir müssen eine Menge Lebensmittel kaufen.

carrot die Karotte
The carrots are next to the potatoes.
Die Karotten sind neben den Kartoffeln.

cauliflower der Blumenkohl
Aunt Lizzie makes great cauliflower soup.
Tante Lizzie macht eine tolle Blumenkohl-suppe.

checkout die (Supermarkt-) Kasse
Aunt Lizzie's friend works at the checkout.
Tante Lizzies Freundin arbeitet an der Kasse.

closed geschlossen
The supermarket is closed on Sundays.
Am Sonntag ist der Supermarkt geschlossen.

customer der Kunde, die Kundin
There are a lot of customers on Saturdays.
Am Samstag sind viele Kunden da.

entrance der Eingang
A customer is pushing a trolley through the entrance door.
Eine Kundin schiebt einen Einkaufswagen durch die Eingangstür.

Shopping

fish der Fisch

Don't forget the fish.
Vergesst nicht den Fisch!

fresh frisch
Fresh today!
Heute frisch!

frozen foods die Tiefkühlkost
It's cold near the frozen foods.
Es ist kalt neben der Tiefkühlkost.

fruit das Obst
Apples, bananas and grapes are fruit.
Äpfel, Bananen und Trauben sind Obst.

to go shopping
einkaufen gehen
The baby loves going shopping.
Das Baby geht gern einkaufen.

handbag die Handtasche
Aunt Lizzie's purse is in her handbag.
Tante Lizzies Geldbeutel ist in ihrer Handtasche.

how much wie viel

How much is it?
Wie viel kostet das?

lettuce der Kopfsalat
Which lettuce shall we buy?
Welchen Kopfsalat sollen wir kaufen?

magazine die Zeitschrift
Aunt Lizzie likes to read magazines.
Tante Lizzie liest gerne Zeitschriften.

Shopping

meat das Fleisch
Mum doesn't like meat.
Mama mag kein Fleisch.

open geöffnet
The supermarket is open today.
Der Supermarkt ist heute geöffnet.

money das Geld
Aunt Lizzie's money is in her purse.
Tante Lizzies Geld ist in ihrem Geldbeutel.

to pay zahlen
We pay for the shopping at the checkout.
Wir zahlen für den Einkauf an der Kasse.

to need brauchen
What do we need today?
Was brauchen wir heute?

plastic Plastik
We can get plastic bags at the checkout.
Wir können Plastiktüten an der Kasse bekommen.

newspaper die Zeitung
Don't forget Uncle Bill's newspaper.
Vergesst Onkel Bills Zeitung nicht!

potato die Kartoffel
Max loves potatoes.
Max liebt Kartoffeln.

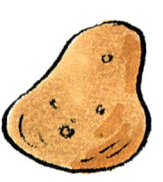

onion die Zwiebel
Onions make me cry.
Zwiebeln bringen mich zum Weinen.

purse der Geldbeutel
Can you see Aunt Lizzie's purse?
Siehst du Tante Lizzies Geldbeutel?

Shopping

to push drücken, schieben
   Aunt Lizzie is pushing the trolley.
   Tante Lizzie schiebt den Einkaufswagen.

tin die Dose
   Can you see the tins of cat food?
   Kannst du die Dosen mit dem Katzenfutter sehen?

shop assistant der Verkaufer, die Verkäuferin
   The shop assistant is working at the checkout.
   Die Verkäuferin arbeitet an der Kasse.

trolley der Einkaufswagen
   The baby likes to sit in the trolley.
   Das Baby sitzt gern im Einkaufswagen.

shopping list die Einkaufsliste
   Where's my shopping list?
   Wo ist meine Einkaufsliste?

vegetable das Gemüse
   Potatoes, carrots and cauliflower are vegetables.
   Kartoffeln, Karotten und Blumenkohl sind Gemüse.

supermarket der Supermarkt
   I'm at the supermarket with Aunt Lizzie.
   Ich bin mit Tante Lizzie im Supermarkt.

to think denken, glauben, meinen
   I think we need lots of pizzas.
   Ich glaube, wir brauchen viele Pizzas.

In the town

motorbike

bridge

river

bus stop

car

fountain

telephone box

letterbox

zebra crossing

ambulance

fire engine

traffic lights

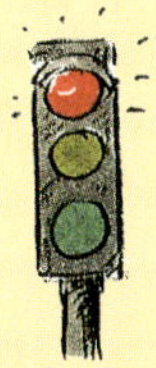

market stall

bench

bus

swing

In the town

ambulance der Krankenwagen
The ambulance is going as fast as lightning.
Der Krankenwagen fährt schnell wie der Blitz.

bakery die Bäckerei
What can you buy at the bakery?
Was kann man in der Bäckerei kaufen?

bank die Bank
Holly's dad works at the bank.
Hollys Papa arbeitet bei der Bank.

bench die Parkbank
Grandma likes to sit on the park bench.
Oma sitzt gern auf der Parkbank.

bridge die Brücke
You can walk over the river on the bridge.
Du kannst auf der Brücke über den Fluss gehen.

building das Gebäude
There are lots of big buildings in the town.
Es gibt viele große Gebäude in der Stadt.

bus der Bus
I like to sit upstairs on the bus.
Ich sitze gern oben im Bus.

bus driver der Busfahrer
The bus driver is wearing a uniform.
Der Busfahrer trägt eine Uniform.

bus stop die Bushaltestelle
There are lots of children at the bus stop.
An der Bushaltestelle sind viele Kinder.

car das Auto
We have a big, silver, family car.
Wir haben ein großes, silbernes Familienauto.

In the town

chemist's die Apotheke
You can get medicine at the chemist's.
Medizin bekommt man in der Apotheke.

church die Kirche
The church bells ring every morning.
Jeden Morgen läuten die Kirchenglocken.

cinema das Kino
Grandma and Grandpa go to the cinema every week.
Oma und Opa gehen jede Woche ins Kino.

corner die Ecke
The red telephone box is on the corner.
Die rote Telefonzelle steht an der Ecke.

to drive fahren
Dad drives to work.
Papa fährt zur Arbeit.

every jeden
The swimming pool is open every day.
Das Hallenbad hat jeden Tag geöffnet.

fire engine das Feuerwehrauto
Jake's dad drives a fire engine.
Jakes Papa fährt ein Feuerwehrauto.

fountain der Brunnen
The ducks are having a shower under the fountain.
Die Enten duschen im Brunnen.

to get on einsteigen
Lots of children are getting on the bus.
Viele Kinder steigen in den Bus ein.

hospital das Krankenhaus
The ambulance is going to the hospital.
Der Krankenwagen fährt zum Krankenhaus.

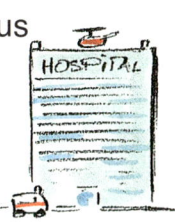

In the town

left links
We drive on the left in England.
In England fährt man auf der linken Straßenseite.

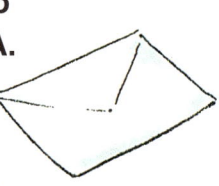

letter der Brief
I'm writing a letter to my friend in the USA.
Ich schreibe gerade einen Brief an meine Freundin in den USA.

letterbox der Briefkasten
I'll put it in the letterbox tomorrow.
Ich werde ihn morgen in den Briefkasten werfen.

lorry der Lastwagen
The lorry has stopped at the zebra crossing.
Der Lastwagen hat vor dem Zebrastreifen angehalten.

market stall der Marktstand
There are two market stalls in front of the church.
Vor der Kirche sind zwei Marktstände.

motorcycle das Motorrad
The motorcycle is next to the lorry.
Das Motorrad steht neben dem Lastwagen.

museum das Museum
Where is the museum?
Wo ist das Museum?

park der Park
The playground is in the park.
Der Spielplatz ist im Park.

pavement der Bürgersteig
Please walk on the pavement, not on the street.
Bitte geh auf dem Bürgersteig und nicht auf der Straße.

In the town

petrol (BE) das Benzin
  Dad's car needs a lot of petrol.
  Papas Auto verbraucht viel Benzin.

petrol station (BE) die Tankstelle
  Dad goes to the petrol station every Friday.
  Papa fährt jeden Freitag zur Tankstelle.

playground der Spielplatz
  It's fun to go to the playground.
  Es macht Spaß, zum Spielplatz zu gehen.

police officer
der Polizist, die Polizistin
  The police officers are in the police car.
  Die Polizisten sitzen im Polizeiauto.

pond der Teich
  Be careful! Don't fall into the duck pond.
  Vorsicht! Fall nicht in den Ententeich.

post office das Postamt
  The letter box is outside the post office.
  Der Briefkasten ist vor dem Postamt.

quiet ruhig, still, leise
  Shh! Be quiet in the museum.
  Psst! Sei leise im Museum.

restaurant das Restaurant
  Grandpa and Grandma like to go to the restaurant.
  Opa und Oma gehen gern ins Restaurant.

right rechts
  Go right at the traffic lights.
  An der Ampel rechts.
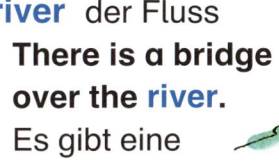

river der Fluss
  There is a bridge over the river.
  Es gibt eine Brücke über den Fluss.

In the town

to sell verkaufen
Can you see the lady selling flowers?
Siehst du die Frau, die Blumen verkauft?

shop der Laden
Mum's favourite shop is the book shop.
Die Buchhandlung ist Mamas Lieblingsladen.

sign das Schild
Where is the sign to the hospital?
Wo ist das Schild zum Krankenhaus?

stamp die Briefmarke
You can buy stamps at the post office.
Briefmarken kannst du im Postamt kaufen.

station der Bahnhof
The trains stop at the station.
Die Züge halten am Bahnhof an.

to stop anhalten
Don't forget to stop at the zebra crossing.
Vergiss nicht, am Zebrastreifen anzuhalten.

street die Straße
There are lots of people in the street.
Es sind viele Menschen auf der Straße.

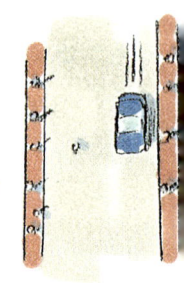

swimming pool das Schwimmbad
We sometimes go to the swimming pool on Saturdays.
Manchmal gehen wir samstags ins Schwimmbad.

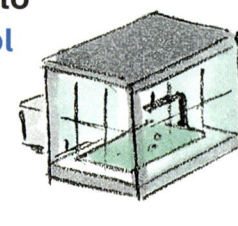

swing die Schaukel
Mia likes to play on the swing.
Mia schaukelt gern.

taxi das Taxi
The taxis are waiting in front of the station.
Die Taxis warten vor dem Bahnhof.

In the town

telephone box die Telefonzelle
There's an old man in the telephone box.
Da ist ein alter Mann in der Telefonzelle.

town die Stadt
Do you live in a town?
Wohnst du in einer Stadt?

town hall das Rathaus
Can you see the town hall clock?
Siehst du die Rathausuhr?

traffic der Verkehr
Is there a lot of traffic in your town?
Ist viel Verkehr in deiner Stadt?

traffic lights die Ampel
What colour are the traffic lights?
Welche Farbe zeigt die Ampel?

train der Zug
We sometimes take the train to London.
Manchmal fahren wir mit dem Zug nach London.

village das Dorf
There's a small village behind our town.
Hinter unserer Stadt ist ein kleines Dorf.

zebra crossing der Zebrastreifen
The traffic has stopped at the zebra crossing.
Der Verkehr hält vor dem Zebrastreifen an.

On the farm

fox   sheep

chicken

pig

fence

goat   frog   butterfly   hedgehog

 scarecrow

 cockerel

lamb

 owl

 bat

 mouse

 horse

 rabbit

bucket

 duck

 cow

On the farm

animal das Tier
There are lots of animals on the farm.
Auf dem Bauernhof gibt es viele Tiere.

bird der Vogel
A bird is sitting on the scarecrow's hat.
Ein Vogel sitzt auf dem Hut der Vogelscheuche.

to bark bellen
Queenie is barking at Max.
Queenie bellt Max an.

bucket der Eimer
What is in the bucket?
Was ist im Eimer?

barn die Scheune
Which animals live in the barn?
Welche Tiere leben in der Scheune?

butterfly der Schmetterling
Where is the butterfly?
Wo ist der Schmetterling?

bat die Fledermaus
What are the bats doing?
Was machen die Fledermäuse?

chick das Küken
The little chicks are hiding under the big chicken.
Die kleinen Küken verstecken sich unter dem großen Huhn.

be careful sei vorsichtig
Be careful, Mia! Don't fall in.
Sei vorsichtig, Mia. Fall nicht rein.

chicken das Huhn
The chickens are eating the corn.
Die Hühner fressen den Mais.

On the farm

cockerel der Hahn
The cockerel is very loud. Be quiet, cockerel!
Der Hahn ist sehr laut. Sei leise, Hahn!

corn der Mais
Can you see the corn in the barn?
Siehst du den Mais in der Scheune?

countryside das Land
Do you live in the countryside?
Wohnst du auf dem Land?

cow die Kuh
Buttercup is Uncle Bill's favourite cow.
Buttercup ist Onkel Bills Lieblingskuh.

duck die Ente
The duck is looking to see what's in the bucket.
Die Ente schaut nach, was im Eimer ist.

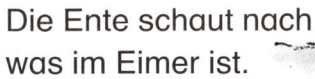

to fall fallen
Max has fallen into the mud.
Max ist in den Matsch gefallen.

farm der Bauernhof
Aunt Lizzie and Uncle Bill live on the farm.
Tante Lizzie und Onkel Bill wohnen auf dem Bauernhof.

farmer der Bauer, die Bäuerin
Uncle Bill is a farmer.
Onkel Bill ist Bauer.

fence der Zaun
The cockerel is sitting on the fence.
Der Hahn sitzt auf dem Zaun.

field das Feld
The scarecrow is in the field.
Die Vogelscheuche steht auf dem Feld.

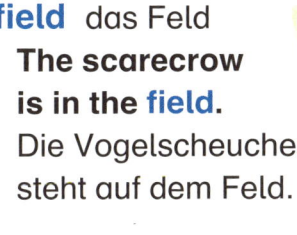

On the farm

fox der Fuchs
The chickens haven't seen the fox.
Die Hühner haben den Fuchs nicht gesehen.

horse das Pferd
The horse loves big green apples.
Das Pferd liebt große grüne Äpfel.

frog der Frosch
The frog is having a bath.
Der Frosch nimmt ein Bad.

lamb das Lamm
The lambs are up on the hill.
Die Lämmer sind oben auf dem Hügel.

goat die Ziege
Mia can't see the goat biting her clothes.
Mia sieht nicht, wie die Ziege ihre Kleider anknabbert.

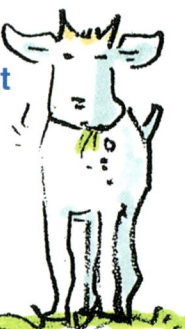

mice die Mäuse
The mice are running in the barn.
Die Mäuse laufen in der Scheune herum.

hedgehog der Igel
The hedgehog is hiding in the barn.
Der Igel versteckt sich in der Scheune.

mouse die Maus
The mouse is eating the corn.
Die Maus frisst den Mais.

hill der Hügel
Aunt Lizzie is driving the tractor up the hill.
Tante Lizzie fährt mit dem Traktor den Hügel hoch.

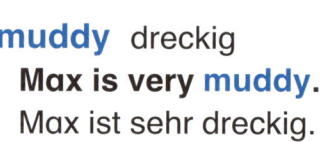

muddy dreckig
Max is very muddy.
Max ist sehr dreckig.

On the farm

nest das Nest
The mice have built their nest in the barn.
Die Mäuse haben ihr Nest in der Scheune gebaut.

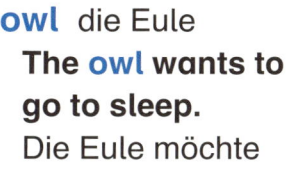

owl die Eule
The owl wants to go to sleep.
Die Eule möchte schlafen.

pig das Schwein
The pig is very muddy, too.
Das Schwein ist auch sehr dreckig.

rabbit das Kaninchen
What colour is the rabbit?
Welche Farbe hat das Kaninchen?

sack der Sack
Can you see the hole in the sack of corn?
Siehst du das Loch im Sack mit Mais?

scarecrow die Vogelscheuche
The birds aren't scared of the scarecrow.
Die Vögel haben keine Angst vor der Vogelscheuche.

sheep das Schaf
The sheep are eating the yummy green grass.
Die Schafe fressen das leckere, grüne Gras.

tractor der Traktor
Aunt Lizzie and the baby are on the tractor.
Tante Lizzie und das Baby sitzen auf dem Traktor.

to watch beobachten
The fox is watching the chickens.
Der Fuchs beobachtet die Hühner.

At the zoo

bear

polar bear

elephant

branch

giraffe

leaf

monkey

gorilla

peacock

snake

crocodile

camel

penguin seal hippo lion

At the zoo

aquarium das Aquarium
There are crocodiles and snakes in the aquarium.
Im Aquarium gibt es Krokodile und Schlangen.

bear der Bär
The brown bear looks like my teddy.
Der braune Bär sieht aus wie mein Teddy.

to bite beißen
Be very careful! The crocodiles bite.
Sei sehr vorsichtig! Die Krokodile beißen.

branch der Ast
The elephant is holding a branch with his trunk.
Der Elefant hält einen Ast mit seinem Rüssel.

café das Café
Let's drink a cup of tea in the café.
Lass uns eine Tasse Tee im Café trinken.

camel das Kamel
A boy is sitting on the camel.
Ein Junge sitzt auf dem Kamel.

to close zumachen, schließen
The zoo keeper mustn't forget to close the cage.
Der Zoowärter darf nicht vergessen den Käfig zuzumachen.

crocodile das Krokodil
The crocodile has lots and lots of teeth.
Das Krokodil hat viele, viele Zähne.

dangerous gefährlich
Be careful! The crocodile's teeth are dangerous.
Vorsicht! Die Zähne vom Krokodil sind gefährlich.

At the zoo

to dream träumen
The lion is dreaming.
Der Löwe träumt.

Tiere nicht füttern!

elephant der Elefant
The elephant is the biggest animal in the zoo.
Der Elefant ist das größte Tier im Zoo.

fishing fischen
The brown bears like to go fishing.
Die Braunbären fischen gern.

fur das Fell
The lion has lovely golden fur.
Der Löwe hat ein wunderschönes goldenes Fell.

excuse me Entschuldigung
Excuse me, I can't see.
Entschuldigung, ich kann nicht sehen.

to feed füttern
The zoo keeper is feeding the tiger.
Der Zoowärter füttert den Tiger.

giraffe die Giraffe
The giraffe has a very, very long neck.
Die Giraffe hat einen sehr, sehr langen Hals.

gorilla der Gorilla
Where are the gorillas?
Wo sind die Gorillas?

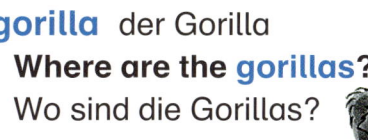

At the zoo

hippo das Nilpferd
Hippos love mud baths.
Nilpferde baden gern im Schlamm.

to hold halten
Mia is holding Grandpa's hand.
Mia hält Opa an der Hand.

insect das Insekt
There's a new insect house in the zoo.
Es gibt ein neues Insektenhaus im Zoo.

jungle der Dschungel
The tiger wants to be in the jungle.
Der Tiger wäre gern im Dschungel.

kangaroo das Känguru
Where do kangaroos come from?
Woher kommen Kängurus?

leaf das Blatt

This leaf tastes yummy.
Dieses Blatt schmeckt lecker.

leaves die Blätter
The giraffe wants to eat the young, green leaves.
Die Giraffe will die jungen, grünen Blätter fressen.

let's lass uns
Let's come to the zoo again tomorrow.
Lass uns morgen noch mal in den Zoo gehen.

lion der Löwe
The lion is very old.
Der Löwe ist sehr alt.

lizard die Eidechse
Lizards love to lie in the sun.
Eidechsen lieben es, in der Sonne zu liegen.

At the zoo

monkey der Affe
The monkeys are angry with the giraffe.
Die Affen sind böse auf die Giraffe.

of course natürlich
Do you like the zoo? Of course.
Magst du den Zoo? Natürlich.

panda der Panda
Do you know where pandas usually live?
Weißt du, wo Pandas normalerweise leben?

pardon? wie bitte?
Pardon? Can you say that again, please?
Wie bitte? Kannst du das bitte noch mal sagen?

parrot der Papagei
The parrots are very loud!
Die Papageien sind sehr laut!

paw die Pfote
Look at the lion's big paws.
Schau dir die großen Pfoten des Löwen an.

peacock der Pfau
The peacock thinks that he is lovely.
Der Pfau glaubt, dass er wunderschön ist.

penguin der Pinguin
The penguins look very funny when they walk.
Die Pinguine sehen beim Gehen sehr lustig aus.

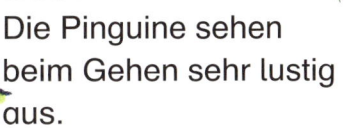

polar bear der Eisbär
The polar bears are swimming in their pool.
Die Eisbären schwimmen in ihrem Becken.

to queue anstellen
Hier anstellen!

At the zoo

race das Wettrennen
The giant tortoises are having a race.
Die Riesenschildkröten machen ein Wettrennen.

ready bereit
We're ready to go.
Wir sind bereit zu gehen.

to roar brüllen
The tiger can roar very loudly.
Der Tiger kann sehr laut brüllen.

to ride reiten
Do you want to ride on the camel?
Möchtest du auf dem Kamel reiten?

seal der Seehund
The seals have fun catching fish.
Die Seehunde haben Spaß beim Fischefangen.

sign post der Wegweiser
The sign post will help us to find the gorillas.
Der Wegweiser wird uns helfen, die Gorillas zu finden.

snake die Schlange
Grandma doesn't like snakes.
Oma mag keine Schlangen.

tiger der Tiger
The tiger is very hungry.
Der Tiger ist sehr hungrig.

trunk der Rüssel
How long is the elephant's trunk?
Wie lang ist der Rüssel des Elefanten?

understand verstehen
The elephant doesn't understand English.
Der Elefant versteht kein Englisch.

At the zoo

unicorn das Einhorn
There isn't a unicorn in the zoo.
Es gibt kein Einhorn im Zoo.

What's the matter?
Was ist los?

yuck! Igitt!

Yuck! Old fish for lunch.
Igitt! Alte Fische zum Mittagessen.

yummy lecker

Mmm. Yummy children.
Mmm. Leckere Kinder.

zebra das Zebra
The zebras look like they are wearing pyjamas.
Die Zebras sehen aus, als ob sie Schlafanzüge tragen.

zoo der Zoo
We're at the zoo with our grandparents.
Wir sind mit unseren Großeltern im Zoo.

zoo keeper der Zoowärter
The zoo keeper must be very careful.
Der Zoowärter muss sehr vorsichtig sein.

At the fairground

roller coaster

vampire

witch

ghost

monster

ticket

bouncy castle

clown

big wheel

helter skelter

bumper car

carousel

candy floss

magic wand

magician

cowboy

At the fairground

again noch mal, wieder
Mia doesn't want to go on the ghost train again.
Mia will nicht noch mal mit der Geisterbahn fahren.

any irgendein
We haven't any money.
Wir haben kein Geld.

big wheel (Ferris wheel) das Riesenrad
We can see our house from the big wheel.
Wir können unser Haus vom Riesenrad aus sehen.

bin der Mülleimer
Throw your rubbish in the bin.
Wirf deinen Müll in den Mülleimer.

bouncy castle die Hüpfburg
Uncle Bill was on the bouncy castle with the baby.
Onkel Bill war mit dem Baby auf der Hüpfburg.

bumper car der Autoskooter
Max wants to go on the bumper cars next.
Max will als Nächstes Autoskooter fahren.

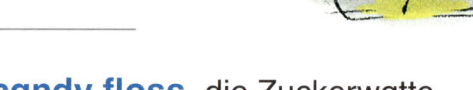

candy floss die Zuckerwatte
The baby loves candy floss.
Das Baby liebt Zuckerwatte.

carousel das Karussell
The horses on the carousel go up and down.
Die Karusselpferde gehen hoch und runter.

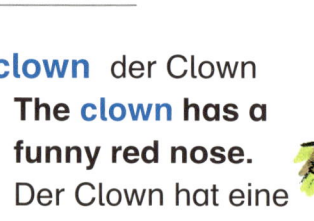

clown der Clown
The clown has a funny red nose.
Der Clown hat eine lustige rote Nase.

At the fairground

cowboy der Cowboy
The **cowboy** is working on the carousel.
Der Cowboy arbeitet auf dem Karussell.

fairground der Rummelplatz
There's lots to do at the **fairground**.
Auf dem Rummelplatz gibt es viel zu tun.

first erste
Max and Mia are in the **first** car.
Max und Mia sind in dem ersten Wagen.

ghost das Gespenst, der Geist
Mia is scared of the **ghost**.
Mia hat Angst vor dem Gespenst.

ghost train die Geisterbahn
Mum doesn't want to go on the **ghost train**.
Mama will nicht mit der Geisterbahn fahren.

to go gehen
Shall we **go to** the fair again tomorrow?
Sollen wir morgen noch mal zu dem Rummelplatz gehen?

to have fun Spaß haben
We're **having** lots of **fun** at the fairground.
Wir haben eine Menge Spaß auf dem Rummelplatz.

helter skelter die Riesenrutsche
Mia wants to go on the **helter skelter**.
Mia will auf die Riesenrutsche.

hot dog der Hotdog
Do you want a **hot dog**?
Willst du einen Hotdog?

to jump hüpfen, springen
The baby likes **jumping** on the bouncy castle.
Das Baby hüpft gerne auf der Hüpfburg.

115

At the fairground

last letzte
  The monster is sitting in the last car.
  Das Monster sitzt in dem letzten Wagen.

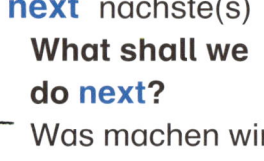

next nächste(s)
  What shall we do next?
  Was machen wir als Nächstes?

magic die Zauberei
  The magician went to a magic school.
  Der Zauberer ging zu einer Zauberschule.

people die Menschen, die Leute
  There are lots of people at the fairground.
  Auf dem Rummelplatz sind viele Leute.

magician der Zauberer
  What is the magician doing?
  Was macht der Zauberer?

pick up aufheben
  Pick up your rubbish, please.
  Heb bitte deinen Müll auf.

magic wand der Zauberstab
  The magician can't find his magic wand.
  Der Zauberer kann seinen Zauberstab nicht finden.

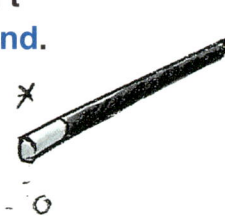

prize der Preis
  Uncle Bill hasn't won a prize this year.
  Onkel Bill hat dieses Jahr keinen Preis gewonnen.

monster das Monster
  Is there a monster under your bed?
  Gibt es ein Monster unter deinem Bett?

queue die Menschenschlange
  There's a long queue for the ghost train.
  Vor der Geisterbahn ist eine lange Menschenschlange.

At the fairground

roller coaster die Achterbahn
Dad and I want to go on the roller coaster.
Papa und ich wollen Achterbahn fahren.

vampire der Vampir
The vampire has blood on his teeth.
Der Vampir hat Blut an den Zähnen.

show die Vorstellung
The next magic show is at two o'clock.
Die nächste Zaubervorstellung ist um zwei Uhr.

to wait warten
Mum and Dad are waiting for the twins.
Mama und Papa warten auf die Zwillinge.

to slide rutschen
I love sliding down the helter skelter.
Ich liebe es, die Riesenrutsche runter zu rutschen.

to win gewinnen
Uncle Bill is trying to win a goldfish.
Onkel Bill versucht, einen Goldfisch zu gewinnen.

witch die Hexe
Queenie doesn't like the witch.
Queenie mag die Hexe nicht.

sticky klebrig
The candy floss is very sticky.
Die Zuckerwatte ist sehr klebrig.

ticket die Fahrkarte
Don't forget to buy a ticket.
Vergiss nicht, eine Fahrkarte zu kaufen.

Around the year

cloud
kite
mummy
pumpkin
lightning
sunflower
rainbow

calendar

snowflakes

rain

umbrella

Easter bunny

Easter egg

daisy

daffodil

Around the year

to be cold frieren
Queenie's paws are very cold.
Queenie friert an den Pfoten.

daffodils die Osterglocken
Mia gave Grandma ten daffodils.
Mia hat Oma zehn Osterglocken geschenkt.

calendar der Kalender
There's a calendar hanging on our kitchen wall.
An unserer Küchenwand hängt ein Kalender.

daisy das Gänseblümchen
Lady Slow is eating the daisy.
Lady Slow frisst das Gänseblümchen.

cloud die Wolke
Can you see the big, black, rain cloud?
Siehst du die große schwarze Regenwolke?

diary das Tagebuch
I try to write in my diary every day.
Ich versuche, jeden Tag in mein Tagebuch zu schreiben.

cloudy bewölkt
It's very cloudy today.
Es ist heute sehr bewölkt.

to dress up sich verkleiden
We always dress up for Halloween.
Wir verkleiden uns immer an Halloween.

cold kalt
My nose is cold.
Meine Nase ist kalt.

Easter Ostern
Easter is in March or April.
Ostern ist im März oder April.

Around the year

Easter bunny der Osterhase
  The **Easter bunny** has hidden the chocolate eggs.
  Der Osterhase hat die Ostereier versteckt.

Easter egg das Osterei
  Max has eaten too many chocolate Easter eggs.
  Max hat zu viele Schokoladenostereier gegessen.

fireworks das Feuerwerk
  In England we have fireworks on the fifth of November.
  In England gibt es am fünften November überall Feuerwerk.

fog der Nebel
  I can't see Queenie in the fog.
  Ich kann Queenie im Nebel nicht sehen.

to forget vergessen
  Don't forget my birthday.
  Vergiss meinen Geburtstag nicht!

Halloween Halloween
  Halloween is on October 31st.
  Halloween ist am 31. Oktober.

Happy New Year!
  Frohes Neues Jahr!

kite der Drachen
  Can you fly a kite?
  Kannst du einen Drachen steigen lassen?

light hell
  What time does it get light in the summer?
  Um welche Uhrzeit wird es im Sommer hell?

lightning der Blitz
  The lightning is very bright.
  Der Blitz ist sehr hell.

Around the year

month der Monat
It's my birthday next month.
Ich habe nächsten Monat Geburtstag.

mummy die Mumie
Max is dressed up as a mummy.
Max hat sich als Mumie verkleidet.

New Year's Eve Silvester
We're having a New Year's Eve party tomorrow.
Morgen feiern wir eine Silvesterparty.

o'clock Uhr (als Zeitangabe)
In the summer it's light at 6 o'clock in the morning.
Im Sommer ist es um 6 Uhr morgens hell.

puddle die Pfütze
Jumping in puddles is lots of fun.
In Pfützen zu hüpfen macht viel Spaß.

pumpkin der Kürbis
Can you see the Halloween pumpkin?
Siehst du den Halloweenkürbis?

rain der Regen
I'm singing in the rain.
Ich singe im Regen.

to rain regnen
I think it's going to rain.
Ich glaube, es wird regnen.

rainbow der Regenbogen
How many colours are in a rainbow?
Wie viele Farben hat ein Regenbogen?

raincoat der Regenmantel
I like wearing my yellow raincoat.
Ich trage meinen gelben Regenmantel gern.

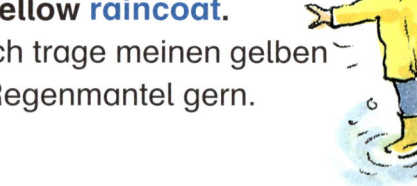

Around the year

school holidays die Schulferien
  We love school holidays.
  Wir lieben die Schulferien.

season die Jahreszeit
  My favourite season is spring.
  Meine Lieblingsjahreszeit ist der Frühling.

skiing Ski laufen
  I sometimes go skiing in winter.
  Manchmal laufe ich im Winter Ski.

sky der Himmel
  The sky is very blue today.
  Der Himmel ist heute sehr blau.

snowball der Schneeball
  Max has made lots of snowballs.
  Max hat viele Schneebälle gemacht.

snowboard das Snowboard
  Max got a snowboard for Christmas.
  Max hat ein Snowboard zu Weihnachten bekommen.

snowflake die Schneeflocke
  Queenie likes catching snowflakes.
  Queenie fängt gerne Schneeflocken.

to splash nass spritzen
  Queenie doesn't like getting splashed.
  Queenie mag es nicht, wenn man sie nass spritzt.

storm der Sturm
  Winston stays inside the house during the storm.
  Während des Sturms bleibt Winston im Haus.

sun die Sonne
  The sun is hiding behind the clouds.
  Die Sonne versteckt sich hinter den Wolken.

Around the year

sunflower die Sonnenblume
The sunflower is as big as me.
Die Sonnenblume ist so groß wie ich.

sunny sonnig
Mum likes long, sunny, summer days.
Mama mag lange sonnige Sommertage.

sunshine der Sonnenschein
Winston loves sleeping in the sunshine.
Winston schläft gern im Sonnenschein.

thunderstorm das Gewitter
Don't fly your kite in a thunderstorm.
Lass deinen Drachen nicht bei einem Gewitter steigen!

umbrella der Regenschirm
Take your umbrella with you when it rains.
Nimm deinen Regenschirm mit, wenn es regnet.

weather das Wetter
What's the weather like today?
Wie ist das Wetter heute?

week die Woche
A week always has seven days.
Eine Woche hat immer sieben Tage.

weekend das Wochenende
Saturday and Sunday are the weekend.
Samstag und Sonntag sind das Wochenende.

wind der Wind
The wind is blowing the leaves off the trees.
Der Wind bläst die Blätter vom Baum.

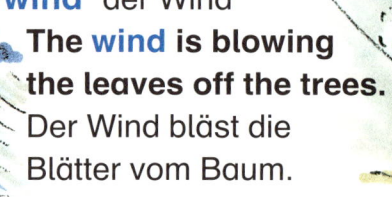

year das Jahr
There are twelve months in a year.
Ein Jahr hat zwölf Monate.

Around the year

days	die Tage
Monday	Montag
Tuesday	Dienstag
Wednesday	Mittwoch
Thursday	Donnerstag
Friday	Freitag
Saturday	Samstag
Sunday	Sonntag
yesterday	gestern
today	heute
tomorrow	morgen

seasons	die Jahreszeiten
spring	der Frühling
summer	der Sommer
autumn	der Herbst
winter	der Winter

months	die Monate
January	Januar
February	Februar
March	März
April	April
May	Mai
June	Juni
July	Juli
August	August
September	September
October	Oktober
November	November
December	Dezember

On holiday

postcard

hotel

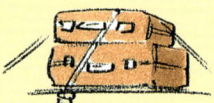
suitcase

camera

flag

sandcastle

crab

sunglasses

spade

seagull whale ship plane

island

lifeguard

lighthouse

seashell jellyfish starfish dolphin

On holiday

beach der Strand
There are lots of great beaches in England.
Es gibt in England viele tolle Strände.

beach towel das Badehandtuch
Mum's sitting on a beach towel.
Mama sitzt auf einem Badehandtuch.

bikini der Bikini
I'm wearing my bikini.
Ich trage meinen Bikini.

boat das Boot
The people in the boat are watching the dolphin.
Die Menschen im Boot beobachten den Delfin.

to build bauen
The twins and I are building a sand castle.
Die Zwillinge und ich bauen eine Sandburg.

camera der Fotoapparat
Dad has his camera round his neck.
Papa hat seinen Fotoapparat um den Hals hängen.

castle das Schloss, die Burg
Yesterday we went to the old castle.
Gestern sind wir zum alten Schloss gegangen.

cave die Höhle
Who is hiding inside the dark cave?
Wer hat sich in der Höhle versteckt?

crab die Krabbe
Ouch! Mia has a crab inside her swimming costume.
Aua! Mia hat eine Krabbe in ihrem Badeanzug.

On holiday

dolphin der Delfin
  The dolphin is jumping out of the water.
  Der Delfin springt aus dem Wasser.

to enjoy genießen
  Dad always enjoys the summer holidays.
  Papa genießt immer die Sommerferien.

flag die Fahne, Flagge
  We put a flag on top of our sand castle.
  Wir stecken eine Flagge in unsere Sandburg.

to fly fliegen
  I'd like to fly like the seagulls.
  Ich möchte wie die Möwen fliegen.

forest der Wald
  The castle is in the middle of the forest.
  Das Schloss ist mitten im Wald.

France Frankreich
  Next year we're going to France.
  Nächstes Jahr fahren wir nach Frankreich.

to go on holiday in Urlaub fahren
  We're going on a summer holiday.
  Wir fahren in den Sommerurlaub.

holiday der Urlaub
  Holidays at the beach are great fun.
  Strandurlaube machen großen Spaß.

hot heiß
  The sand is very hot.
  Der Sand ist sehr heiß.

hotel das Hotel
  We're staying in the Beach Hotel.
  Wir bleiben im Beach Hotel.

On holiday

ice cream shop die Eisdiele
  Dad's gone to the ice cream shop.
  Papa ist zur Eisdiele gegangen.

idea die Idee
  Max has an idea.
  Max hat eine Idee.

island die Insel
  I'd like to live on the island.
  Ich möchte auf der Insel wohnen.

jellyfish die Qualle
  Don't eat the jellyfish, Queenie!
  Nicht die Qualle fressen, Queenie!

to keep halten, behalten
  The cap keeps the sun off Max's head.
  Der Mütze hält die Sonne von Max' Kopf fern.

lifeguard der Rettungsschwimmer
  The lifeguard is watching the people in the sea.
  Der Rettungsschwimmer beobachtet die Leute im Meer.

lighthouse der Leuchtturm
  There's a lighthouse on the island.
  Auf der Insel gibt es einen Leuchtturm.

picnic das Picknick
  We're having a picnic for lunch.
  Wir machen mittags ein Picknick.

pirate der Pirat
  The pirate is inside the dark cave.
  Der Pirat ist in der dunklen Höhle.

On holiday

plane (aeroplane) das Flugzeug
The people in the plane are going on holiday, too.
Die Leute im Flugzeug fliegen auch in Urlaub.

post card die Postkarte
I wrote a post card to Holly yesterday.
Gestern habe ich eine Postkarte an Holly geschrieben.

put stellen, legen, setzen
Put your sun hat on!
Setz deinen Sonnenhut auf!

to relax sich entspannen
Mum wants to relax on the beach.
Mama will sich am Strand entspannen.

rock der Fels
The seals are sitting on the rocks.
Die Seehunde sitzen auf den Felsen.

sand der Sand
It's fun to play in the sand.
Es macht Spaß, im Sand zu spielen.

sandcastle die Sandburg
I think our sandcastle is great!
Ich finde, unsere Sandburg ist toll!

sandwich das Sandwich

Yuck! I have sand in my sandwich.
Igitt! Ich habe Sand in meinem Sandwich.

sea das Meer
The sea is too cold for Dad.
Das Meer ist zu kalt für Papa.

seagull die Möwe
The seagull's feet are in the sea.
Die Möwe steht mit ihren Füßen im Meer.

On holiday

seahorse das Seepferdchen
Aah, don't the seahorses look sweet?
Aah, sehen die Seepferdchen nicht süß aus?

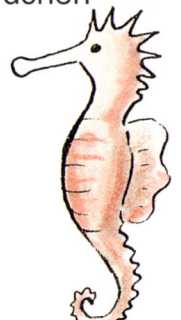

seashell die Muschel
We found pink seashells on the beach.
Wir haben rosa Muscheln am Strand gefunden.

shark der Hai
It's not a good idea to go swimming with sharks.
Es ist keine gute Idee, mit Haien zu schwimmen.

ship das Schiff
The big ship is going to France.
Das große Schiff fährt nach Frankreich.

spade die Schaufel
You need a bucket and spade to make a good sand castle.
Du brauchst eine Schaufel und einen Eimer, um eine gute Sandburg zu bauen.

starfish der Seestern
How many arms has the starfish?
Wie viele Arme hat der Seestern?

to stay bleiben
We're staying here for a week.
Wir bleiben eine Woche hier.

steps die Treppe
The steps go from the street to the beach.
Die Treppe führt von der Straße zum Strand.

stone der Stein
Is there a crab hiding under the stone?
Versteckt sich da eine Krabbe unter dem Stein?

On holiday

suitcase der Koffer
Our suitcases are on the roof of the car.
Unsere Koffer sind auf dem Dach des Autos.

sunglasses die Sonnenbrille
I'm wearing my sunglasses.
Ich trage meine Sonnenbrille.

suntan lotion die Sonnencreme
Don't forget the suntan lotion.
Vergiss die Sonnencreme nicht.

surfboard das Surfbrett
Can you see the boy on his surfboard?
Siehst du den Jungen auf seinem Surfbrett?

to swim schwimmen
There's a man swimming in the sea.
Ein Mann schwimmt im Meer.

swimming costume der Badeanzug
Mia is wearing her favourite swimming costume.
Mia trägt ihren Lieblingsbadeanzug.

swimming trunks die Badehose
Max is wearing his old swimming trunks.
Max trägt seine alte Badehose.

to take photos fotografieren
A man is taking photos.
Ein Mann fotografiert.

treasure der Schatz
The pirate is trying to hide his treasure.
Der Pirat versucht, seinen Schatz zu verstecken.

whale der Wal
Can you see the whale?
Siehst du den Wal?

Birthday

balloon

glass

invitation

birthday cake

jelly

knife

fork

ice cream

candle

birthday card

birthday present

sausage

spoon

plate

cup

Birthday

to bake backen
Grandma baked me a lovely cake.
Oma hat mir einen wunderschönen Kuchen gebacken.

balloon der Luftballon
Winston doesn't like balloons.
Winston mag keine Luftballons.

birthday der Geburtstag
It's my birthday today.
Heute habe ich Geburtstag.

birthday cake der Geburtstagskuchen
The jelly is next to the birthday cake.
Der Wackelpudding steht neben dem Geburtstagskuchen.

birthday card die Geburtstagskarte
Lots of birthday cards came for me this morning.
Heute Morgen sind viele Geburtstagskarten für mich gekommen.

birthday party die Geburtstagsparty
I'm having a birthday party this afternoon.
Heute Nachmittag feiere ich eine Geburtstagsparty.

birthday present das Geburtstagsgeschenk
I got lots of lovely birthday presents.
Ich habe viele schöne Geburtstagsgeschenke bekommen.

to blow out ausblasen
The birthday child can blow out the candles.
Das Geburtstagskind darf die Kerzen ausblasen.

Birthday

candle die Kerze
How many candles are on the cake?
Wie viele Kerzen sind auf dem Kuchen?

to give geben, schenken
Mum and Dad gave me a bike.
Mama und Papa haben mir ein Fahrrad geschenkt.

cola (coke®) die Cola
There's a big bottle of cola on the table.
Auf dem Tisch steht eine große Flasche Cola.

glass das Glas

Do you want a glass of cola?
Willst du ein Glas Cola?

cup die Tasse
Grandma's drinking a cup of tea.
Oma trinkt eine Tasse Tee.

Happy birthday!
Herzlichen Glückwunsch zum Geburtstag!

fork die Gabel
Grandma is eating her cake with a fork.
Oma isst ihren Kuchen mit einer Gabel.

ice cream das Eis
We have chocolate ice cream and strawberry ice cream.
Es gibt Schokoladeneis und Erdbeereis.

to get bekommen
What did you get for your birthday?
Was hast du zum Geburtstag bekommen?

Birthday

invitation die Einladung
I gave party invitations to my friends.
Ich habe Einladungen zu meiner Party an meine Freunde verteilt.

to invite einladen
I've invited Holly and Jake to my birthday party.
Ich habe Holly und Jake zu meiner Geburtstagsparty eingeladen.

jelly der Wackelpudding
Do you like green jelly?
Magst du grünen Wackelpudding?

knife das Messer
The knives are next to the forks.
Die Messer sind neben den Gabeln.

lemonade die Limonade
There's a big bottle of lemonade, too.
Es gibt auch eine große Flasche Limonade.

to make a wish sich etwas wünschen
Blow out the candles, and make a wish.
Blas die Kerzen aus und wünsch dir was.

plate der Teller

Don't run with your plate.
Renn nicht mit deinem Teller herum.

please bitte
Please come to my party.
Bitte komm zu meiner Party.

Birthday

sausage das Würstchen
Queenie loves sausages.
Queenie liebt Würstchen.

serviette die Serviette
The red serviettes are on the table.
Die roten Servietten sind auf dem Tisch.

spoon der Löffel
Where are the spoons?
Wo sind die Löffel?

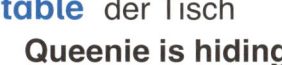

table der Tisch
Queenie is hiding under the table.
Queenie versteckt sich unterm Tisch.

tablecloth das Tischtuch
The tablecloth is on the table.
Das Tischtuch ist auf dem Tisch.

thank you Danke schön

Thank you for my birthday presents.
Danke für meine Geburtstagsgeschenke.

thank you very much vielen Dank

Thank you very much.
Vielen Dank.

very sehr
I'm very happy.
Ich bin sehr glücklich.

wrapping paper das Geschenkpapier
The presents were in wrapping paper.
Die Geschenke waren in Geschenkpapier eingepackt.

Christmas

angel

mistletoe

Christmas tree

Father Christmas, Santa Claus

sleigh

reindeer

Christmas cracker

fire place

snowman

robin

Christmas pudding

holly

turkey  present stocking paper hat

141

Christmas

angel der Engel
We put an angel on the top of the Christmas tree.
Wir setzten einen Engel oben auf den Weihnachtsbaum.

Christmas Weihnachten
Christmas is one of my favourite times of the year.
Weihnachten ist eine meiner Lieblingszeiten im Jahr.

badminton Federball
Mum gave me a badminton set for Christmas.
Mama schenkte mir ein Federballspiel zu Weihnachten.

Christmas card die Weihnachtskarte
People in England always write a lot of Christmas cards.
Die Leute in England schreiben immer viele Weihnachtskarten.

cake der Kuchen
The cake tastes yummy!
Der Kuchen schmeckt lecker.

Christmas carol das Weihnachtslied
Children go from house to house and sing Christmas carols.
Die Kinder gehen von Haus zu Haus und singen Weihnachtslieder.

to celebrate feiern
We celebrate Christmas on the twenty-fifth of December.
Weihnachten feiern wir am fünfundzwanzigsten Dezember.

Christmas cracker der Knallbonbon
What's inside your Christmas cracker?
Was ist in deinem Knallbonbon?

Christmas

Christmas Day
der erste Weihnachtstag
We eat our Christmas dinner on Christmas Day.
Wir essen unser Weihnachtsessen am ersten Weihnachtstag.

Christmas tree
der Weihnachtsbaum
The Christmas tree looks lovely.
Der Weihnachtsbaum sieht wunderschön aus.

Christmas Eve Heiligabend
Christmas Eve is on the twenty-fourth of December.
Heiligabend ist am vierundzwanzigsten Dezember.

to decorate schmücken
We helped to decorate the Christmas tree.
Wir haben geholfen, den Weihnachtsbaum zu schmücken.

dessert die Nachspeise
We'll eat the Christmas pudding for dessert.
Wir werden den Plumpudding als Nachspeise essen.

Christmas pudding
der Plumpudding
Aunt Lizzie has decorated the Christmas pudding with holly.
Tante Lizzie hat den Plumpudding mit einem Stechpalmenzweig verziert.

drum die Trommel
Why did Grandpa give the baby a drum?
Warum hat Opa dem Baby eine Trommel geschenkt?

Christmas

Father Christmas (BE)
der Weihnachtsmann
Can you see a picture of Father Christmas?
Siehst du ein Bild vom Weihnachtsmann?

to finish fertig
Are you finished?
Bist du fertig?

fire das Feuer
Uncle Bill has made a lovely fire.
Onkel Bill hat ein wunderschönes Feuer gemacht.

fire place der Kamin
In winter Winston likes to sleep in front of the fire place.
Im Winter schläft Winston gern vor dem Kamin.

gold golden
How many gold balls are there on the Christmas tree?
Wie viele goldene Kugeln hängen am Weihnachtsbaum?

great! toll!
Christmas is great!
Weihnachten ist toll!

to hang hängen
The gold and silver balls are hanging on the Christmas tree.
Die goldenen und silbernen Kugeln hängen am Weihnachtsbaum.

holly die Stechpalme
Don't eat the holly!
Iss nicht die Stechpalme!

ice das Eis
There's ice on the window.
Am Fenster ist Eis.

Christmas

to kiss küssen
Mum and Dad kissed under the mistletoe.
Mama und Papa küssten sich unterm Mistelzweig.

lots of viele
There are lots of presents under the Christmas tree.
Da sind viele Geschenke unterm Weihnachtsbaum.

Merry Christmas!
Frohe Weihnachten!

middle die Mitte
The vegetables are in the middle of the table.
Das Gemüse steht mitten auf dem Tisch.

mistletoe der Mistelzweig
The mistletoe is hanging over the door.
Der Mistelzweig hängt über der Tür.

to open aufmachen, öffnen
Brr, it's cold outside. Don't open the window.
Brr, draußen ist es kalt. Mach das Fenster nicht auf.

paper hat der Papierhut
The paper hats were inside the Christmas crackers.
Die Papierhüte waren in den Knallbonbons.

pea die Erbse
The peas always fall of my fork.
Die Erbsen fallen immer von meiner Gabel.

pepper der Pfeffer

Can I have the pepper, please?
Kann ich bitte den Pfeffer haben?

Christmas

to prefer lieber mögen
  Do you prefer carrots or peas?
  Magst du lieber Karotten oder Erbsen?

present das Geschenk
  Father Christmas puts presents into the children's stockings.
  Der Weihnachtsmann steckt den Kindern Geschenke in ihre Strümpfe.

to pull ziehen
  Pull the Christmas cracker.
  Zieh den Knallbonbon auseinander.

reindeer das Rentier
  Reindeers pull Father Christmas's sleigh.
  Die Rentiere ziehen den Schlitten vom Weihnachtsmann.

to roast braten
  We're having roast turkey for Christmas dinner.
  Bei uns gibt es gebratenen Truthahn zu Weihnachten.

robin das Rotkehlchen
  A robin is looking through the window.
  Ein Rotkehlchen schaut durch das Fenster herein.

salt das Salz
  I like salt on my roast potatoes.
  Ich mag Salz auf meinen Bratkartoffeln.

Santa Claus (AE) der Weihnachtsmann
  In the USA Father Christmas is called Santa Claus.
  In den USA heißt der Weihnachtsmann Santa Claus.

Christmas

to say sagen
What did you say?
Was hast du gesagt?

shiny glänzend
Can you see the shiny balls on the tree?
Siehst du die glänzenden Kugeln am Baum?

silver silber
The Christmas tree is decorated with gold and silver balls.
Der Weihnachtsbaum ist mit goldenen und silbernen Kugeln geschmückt.

sleigh der Schlitten
Father Christmas brings the presents in his sleigh.
Der Weihnachtsmann bringt die Geschenke in seinem Schlitten.

snow der Schnee
There's lots of snow outside.
Draußen liegt viel Schnee.

snowman der Schneemann
Can you see our snowman?
Kannst du unseren Schneemann sehen?

stocking der Strumpf
On Christmas Eve children hang up their stockings.
An Heiligabend hängen die Kinder ihre Strümpfe auf.

turkey der Truthahn
Aunt Lizzie roasted a giant turkey.
Tante Lizzie hat einen riesigen Truthahn gebraten.

Opposites, numbers, colours, shapes, and prepositions

black

blue

brown

dark blue

green   **grey**   **light blue**

circle

rectangle

square

triangle

yellow

white

red

orange

pink

purple

Opposites, numbers, colours, shapes, and prepositions

opposites   Gegensätze

big groß
   Buttercup is big.
   Buttercup ist groß.

small klein
   Furball is small.
   Furball ist klein.

sweet süß
   Sugar is sweet.
   Zucker ist süß.

sour sauer
   Lemons are sour.
   Zitronen sind sauer.

dirty schmutzig
   The baby is dirty.
   Das Baby ist schmutzig.

clean sauber
   Winston is clean.
   Winston ist sauber.

wet nass
   Water is wet.
   Wasser ist nass.

dry trocken
   The towel is dry.
   Das Handtuch ist trocken.

thin dünn
   The snake is thin.
   Die Schlange ist dünn.

fat dick
   The hippo is fat.
   Das Nilpferd ist dick.

long lang
   The giraffe has long legs.
   Die Giraffe hat lange Beine.

short kurz
   Lady Slow has short legs.
   Lady Slow hat kurze Beine.

easy einfach, leicht
   This is easy.
   Das ist einfach.

difficult schwierig
   This is difficult.
   Das ist schwierig.

fast schnell
   The horse is fast.
   Das Pferd ist schnell.

150

Opposites, numbers, colours, shapes, and prepositions

slow langsam
The tortoise is slow.
Die Schildkröte ist langsam.

---

hard hart
The rock is hard.
Der Fels ist hart.

soft weich
The pillow is soft.
Das Kopfkissen ist weich.

right richtig
This answer is right.
Diese Antwort ist richtig.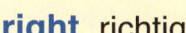

wrong falsch
This answer is wrong.
Diese Antwort ist falsch.

new neu
The car is new.
Das Auto ist neu.

old alt
The tractor is old.
Der Traktor ist alt.

loud laut
My alarm clock is loud.
Mein Wecker ist laut.

quiet leise
The mouse is quiet.
Die Maus ist leise.

---

good gut
That's a good idea.
Das ist eine gute Idee.

bad schlecht
That's a bad idea.
Das ist eine schlechte Idee.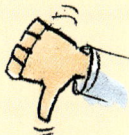

---

full voll
This glass is full.
Dieses Glas ist voll.

empty leer
This glass is empty.
Dieses Glas ist leer.

---

cheap billig
The broken old car is cheap.
Das kaputte alte Auto ist billig.

expensive teuer
The shiny new car is expensive.
Das glänzende neue Auto ist teuer.

Opposites, numbers, colours, shapes, and prepositions

heavy schwer
   Mum's shopping bags are heavy.
   Mamas Einkaufstüten sind schwer.

light leicht
   Mia's rucksack is light.
   Mia's Rucksack ist leicht.

rich reich
   The pirate is rich.
   Der Pirat ist reich.

poor arm
   The old man is poor.
   Der alte Mann ist arm.

eleven	elf
twelve	zwölf
thirteen	dreizehn
fourteen	vierzehn
fifteen	fünfzehn
sixteen	sechzehn
seventeen	siebzehn
eighteen	achtzehn
nineteen	neunzehn
twenty	zwanzig
thirty	dreißig
forty	vierzig
fifty	fünfzig
sixty	sechzig
seventy	siebzig
eighty	achtzig
ninety	neunzig
one hundred	hundert

numbers	die Zahlen
one	eins
two	zwei
three	drei
four	vier
five	fünf
six	sechs
seven	sieben
eight	acht
nine	neun
ten	zehn

colours	die Farben
black	schwarz
blue	blau
brown	braun
dark blue	dunkelblau
green	grün
grey	grau
light blue	hellblau
orange	orange
pink	rosa
purple	lila
red	rot
white	weiß
yellow	gelb

Opposites, numbers, colours, shapes, and prepositions

shapes	Formen
circle	der Kreis
rectangle	das Rechteck
square	das Quadrat
triangle	das Dreieck

prepositions	Präpositionen
about	über, um
above	über
and	und
as	wie
at	an, bei, zu
because	weil
behind	hinter
below	unter
between	zwischen
but	aber
down	hinunter
from	von
in	in
in front of	vor
inside	drinnen
into	in (hinein)
maybe	vielleicht
next to	neben
of	von
off	ab, auf
on	auf
opposite	gegenüber
or	oder
outside	draußen
over	über
round	herum
through	durch
to	zu
under	unter
up	hinauf, hoch
with	mit

pronouns	Pronomen
I	ich
you	du
he	er
she	sie
it	es
we	wir
you	Sie, ihr
they	sie
mine	mein(e)
your	dein(e)
her	ihr(e)
his, its	sein(e)
our	unser(e)
your	euer(e)
their	ihr(e)

question words	Fragewörter
how	wie
how many	wie viel
what	was
when	wann
where	wo
which	welche, -r, -s
who	wer
why	warum

Wörterverzeichnis Englisch – Deutsch

BE bedeutet britisches Englisch, AE amerikanisches Englisch

about [əˈbaʊt] über, um 153
above [əˈbʌv] über 153
address [əˈdres] die Adresse 16
to be afraid of [tə biː əˈfreɪd ɒv] Angst haben vor 38
after [ˈɑːftə] nach 54
afternoon [ˌɑːftəˈnuːn] der Nachmittag 54
again [əˈgen] noch mal 114
to agree [tə əˈgriː] zustimmen 38
alarm clock [əˈlɑːm klɒk] der Wecker 23, 24
alphabet [ˈælfəbet] das Alphabet 62
always [ˈɔːlweɪz] immer 54
am [æm] bin 8
ambulance [ˈæmbjələns] der Krankenwagen 91, 92
and [ænd] und 153
angel [ˈeɪndʒəl] der Engel 140, 142
angry [ˈæŋgrɪ] wütend 38
animal [ˈænɪml] das Tier 100
answer [ˈɑːnsə] die Antwort 62
ant [ænt] die Ameise 98
any [ˈenɪ] irgendein(e), irgendwelche 114
apartment (AE) [əˈpɑːtmənt] die Wohnung 16
apple [ˈæpl] der Apfel 76, 78
April [ˈeɪprəl] April 125
aquarium [əˈkweərɪəm] das Aquarium 106
are [ɑː] sind 8
arm [ɑːm] der Arm 29, 30
armchair [ˈɑːmtʃeə] der Sessel 14, 16
art [ɑːt] Kunst 62
as [æz] wie 153
to ask [tʊ ˈɑːsk] fragen 62
at [æt] an, bei, zu 153
at home [ət ˈhəʊm] zu Hause 16

attic [ˈætɪk] der Dachboden 16
August [ˈɔːgəst] August 125
aunt [ɑːnt] die Tante 8
autumn [ˈɔːtəm] der Herbst 125

baby [ˈbeɪbɪ] das Baby 7, 8
back [bæk] der Rücken 30
bad [bæd] schlecht 151
badminton [ˈbædmɪntən] der Federball 142
bag [bæg] die Tasche 46
to bake [tə ˈbeɪk] backen 136
bakery [ˈbeɪkərɪ] die Bäckerei 92
balcony [ˈbælkənɪ] der Balkon 16
ball [bɔːl] der Ball 22, 24
balloon [bəˈluːn] der Luftballon 134, 136
banana [bəˈnɑːnə] die Banane 77, 78
bandage [ˈbændɪdʒ] der Verband 29, 30
bank [bæŋk] die Bank 92
to bark [tə ˈbɑːk] bellen 100
barn [bɑːn] die Scheune 100
baseball [ˈbeɪsbɔːl] der Baseball 46
basket [ˈbɑːskɪt] der Korb 77, 78
basketball [ˈbɑːskɪtbɔːl] der Basketball 71, 72
bat [bæt] die Fledermaus 99, 100
bath (BE) [bɑːθ] die Badewanne 16
to have a bath [tə hæv ə ˈbɑːθ] baden 33
bathroom [ˈbɑːθruːm] das Badezimmer 16
to be [tə ˈbiː] sein 8
beach [biːtʃ] der Strand 128
beach towel [ˈbiːtʃtaʊəl] das Badehandtuch 128
bean [biːn] die Bohne 78
bear [beə] der Bär 104, 106
beard [bɪəd] der Bart 7, 8

beautiful [ˈbjuːtəfl] schön 38
because [bɪˈkɒz] weil 153
bed [bed] das Bett 24
bedroom [ˈbedruːm] das Schlafzimmer 16
bee [biː] die Biene 14, 16
before [bɪˈfɔː] vor 54
to begin [tə bɪˈgɪn] anfangen 54
behind [bɪˈhaɪnd] hinter 153
to believe [tə bɪˈliːv] glauben 38
bell [bel] die Glocke 60, 62
below [bɪˈləʊ] unter 153
belt [belt] der Gürtel 45, 46
bench [bentʃ] die Parkbank 91, 92
best [best] beste, bester 8
better [ˈbetə] besser 38
between [bɪˈtwiːn] zwischen 153
bicycle [ˈbaɪsɪkl] das Fahrrad 38
big [bɪg] groß 150
big wheel [ˌbɪgˈwiːl] das Riesenrad 113
bike [baɪk] das Fahrrad 38
bikini [bɪˈkiːnɪ] der Bikini 128
bin [bɪn] der Mülleimer 114
bird [bɜːd] der Vogel 100
bird house [ˈbɜːdhaʊs] das Vogelhäuschen 15, 17
birthday [ˈbɜːθdeɪ] der Geburtstag 136
birthday cake [ˈbɜːθdeɪ ˌkeɪk] der Geburtstagskuchen 134, 136
birthday card [ˈbɜːθdeɪ ˌkɑːd] die Geburtstagskarte 135, 136
birthday party [ˈbɜːθdeɪ ˌpɑːtɪ] die Geburtstagsparty 136
birthday present [ˈbɜːθdeɪ ˌpreznt] das Geburtstagsgeschenk 135, 136
biscuit [ˈbɪskɪt] der Keks 78
to bite [tə ˈbaɪt] beißen 106
black [blæk] schwarz 148, 152

Wörterverzeichnis Englisch – Deutsch

blackboard [ˈblækbɔːd] die Tafel 62
blanket [ˈblæŋkɪt] die Decke 46
to bleed [tə ˈbliːd] bluten 30
blonde [blɒnd] blond 30
blouse [blaʊs] die Bluse 46
to blow out [tə ˌbləʊˈaʊt] ausblasen 136
blue [bluː] blau 148, 152
boat [bəʊt] das Boot 128
body [ˈbɒdɪ] der Körper 30
bone [bəʊn] der Knochen 28, 30
book [bʊk] das Buch 60, 62
bookcase [ˈbʊkkeɪs] das Bücherregal 62
boots [buːts] die Stiefel 44, 46
boring [ˈbɔːrɪŋ] langweilig 39
bottle [ˈbɒtl] die Flasche 84, 86
bottom [ˈbɒtəm] der Po, der Hintern 30
bouncy castle [ˈbaʊnsɪˌkɑːsl] die Hüpfburg 112, 114
bowl [bəʊl] die Schüssel, die Schale 78
box [bɒks] die Schachtel 22, 24
boy [bɔɪ] der Junge 7, 8
bracelet [ˈbreɪslət] das Armband 46
branch [brɑːntʃ] der Ast 104, 106
bread [bred] das Brot 84, 86
break [breɪk] die Pause 62
to break [tə ˈbreɪk] kaputt machen 24
breakfast [ˈbrekfəst] das Frühstück 54
to have breakfast [tə hæv ˈbrekfəst] frühstücken 56
bridge [brɪdʒ] die Brücke 90, 92
to bring [tə ˈbrɪŋ] bringen 46
brother [ˈbrʌðə] der Bruder 8
brown [braʊn] braun 148, 152
bruise [bruːz] der blaue Fleck 30

to brush one's teeth [tə ˈbrʌʃ wʌnz ˈtiːθ] sich die Zähne putzen 54
bucket [ˈbʌkɪt] der Eimer 99, 100
to build [tə ˈbɪld] bauen 128
building [ˈbɪldɪŋ] das Gebäude 92
to bump [tə ˈbʌmp] anstoßen 30
bumper car [ˈbʌmpəˌkɑː] der Autoskooter 113, 114
bus [bʌs] der Bus 91, 92
bus driver [ˈbʌsˌdraɪvə] der Busfahrer, die Busfahrerin 92
bus stop [ˈbʌsˌstɒp] die Bushaltestelle 90, 92
bush [bʊʃ] der Busch, der Strauch 14, 17
busy [ˈbɪzɪ] beschäftigt 72
but [bʌt] aber 153
butter [ˈbʌtə] die Butter 78
butterfly [ˈbʌtəflaɪ] der Schmetterling 98, 100
button [ˈbʌtn] der Knopf 45, 46
to buy [tə ˈbaɪ] kaufen 86

C

café [ˈkæfeɪ] das Café 106
cage [keɪdʒ] der Käfig 61, 63
cake [keɪk] der Kuchen 142
calculator [ˈkælkjʊleɪtə] der Taschenrechner 61, 63
calendar [ˈkæləndə] der Kalender 119, 120
to be called [tə bɪ ˈkɔːld] heißen 8
camel [ˈkæml] das Kamel 105, 106
camera [ˈkæmərə] der Fotoapparat 126, 128
can [kæn] können 17, 63
candle [ˈkændl] die Kerze 135, 137
candy floss [ˈkændɪflɒs] die Zuckerwatte 113, 114
cap [kæp] die Mütze 46
car [kɑː] das Auto 92

carousel [kærəˈsel] das Karussell 113, 114
carpet [ˈkɑːpɪt] der Teppich 17
carrot [ˈkærət] die Karotte 86
to carry [tə ˈkærɪ] tragen 78
cassette [kəˈset] die Kassette 24
castle [ˈkɑːsl] das Schloss, die Burg 128
cat [kæt] die Katze, der Kater 7, 8
to catch [tə ˈkætʃ] fangen 72
cauliflower [ˈkɒlɪˌflaʊə] der Blumenkohl 85, 86
cave [keɪv] die Höhle 128
CD [ˌsiːˈdiː] die CD 24
CD player [ˌsiːˈdiːˌpleɪə] der CD-Player 24
to celebrate [tə ˈseləbreɪt] feiern 142
cellar [ˈselə] der Keller 17
chair [tʃeə] der Stuhl 23, 24
chalk [tʃɔːk] die Kreide 63
cheap [tʃiːp] billig 151
checkout [ˈtʃekaʊt] die (Supermarkt-) Kasse 86
cheese [tʃiːz] der Käse 76, 78
chemist's [ˈkemɪsts] die Apotheke 93
chest [tʃest] die Brust 31
chick [tʃɪk] das Küken 100
chicken [ˈtʃɪkɪn] das Huhn 98, 100
child [tʃaɪld] das Kind 9
children [ˈtʃɪldrən] die Kinder 9
chimney [ˈtʃɪmnɪ] der Schornstein 15, 17
chin [tʃɪn] das Kinn 31
chocolate [ˈtʃɒklət] die Schokolade 76, 78
Christmas [ˈkrɪsməs] Weihnachten 142
Christmas card [ˈkrɪsməsˌkɑːd] die Weihnachtskarte 142
Christmas carol [ˈkrɪsməsˈkærəl] das Weihnachtslied 142

155

Wörterverzeichnis Englisch – Deutsch

Christmas cracker [ˈkrɪsməsˈkrækə] das Knallbonbon 140, 142
Christmas Day [ˌkrɪsməsˈdeɪ] der erste Weihnachtsfeiertag 143
Christmas Eve [ˌkrɪsməsˈiːv] Heiligabend 143
Christmas pudding [ˌkrɪsməsˈpʊdɪŋ] der Plumpudding 141, 143
Christmas tree [ˈkrɪsməsˌtriː] der Weihnachtsbaum 140, 143
church [tʃɜːtʃ] die Kirche 93
cinema [ˈsɪnəmə] das Kino 93
circle [ˈsɜːkl] der Kreis 153
classroom [ˈklɑːsruːm] das Klassenzimmer 63
clean [kliːn] sauber 150
clever [ˈklevə] schlau, klug 39
to climb [tə ˈklaɪm] klettern 9
clock [klɒk] die Uhr 52, 55
to close [tə ˈkləʊz] zumachen, schließen 106
closed [kləʊzd] geschlossen 86
clothes [kləʊðz] die Kleidung 47
clothes hanger [ˈkləʊðzˌhæŋə] der Kleiderbügel 44, 47
cloud [klaʊd] die Wolke 118, 120
cloudy [ˈklaʊdɪ] bewölkt 120
clown [klaʊn] der Clown 112, 114
coat [kəʊt] der Mantel 47
cockerel [ˈkɒkərəl] der junge Hahn 99, 101
coffee [ˈkɒfɪ] der Kaffee 79
cola (coke®) [ˈkəʊlə/kəʊk] die Cola 137
cold [kəʊld] kalt 31, 120
cold [kəʊld] die Erkältung 31, 120
to be cold [tə bɪ ˈkəʊld] frieren 120
to collect [tə kəˈlekt] sammeln 72

colours [ˈkʌləz] die Farben 152
to come [tə ˈkʌm] kommen 55
to come from [tə ˈkʌm frɒm] kommen aus 9
comic [ˈkɒmɪk] das Comic-Heft 24
computer [kəmˈpjuːtə] der Computer 25
computer game [kəmˈpjuːtəˌgeɪm] das Computerspiel 25
to cook [tə ˈkʊk] kochen 72
corn [kɔːn] der Mais 101
corner [ˈkɔːnə] die Ecke 93
cough [kɒf] der Husten 31
countryside [ˈkʌntrɪsaɪd] das Land, die Landschaft 17, 101
cousin [ˈkʌzn] der Cousin, die Cousine 9
cow [kaʊ] die Kuh 99, 101
cowboy [ˈkaʊbɔɪ] der Cowboy 113, 115
crab [kræb] die Krabbe 126, 128
cream [kriːm] die Sahne 79
crisps (BE) [krɪsps] die Chips 77, 79
crocodile [ˈkrɒkədaɪl] das Krokodil 105, 106
crown [kraʊn] die Krone 53, 55
to cry [tə ˈkraɪ] weinen 39
cup [kʌp] die Tasse 135, 137
cupboard [ˈkʌbəd] der Schrank 79
curly [ˈkɜːlɪ] lockig 31
curtain [ˈkɜːtn] der Vorhang 14, 17
customer [ˈkʌstəmə] der Kunde, die Kundin 86
to cut [tə ˈkʌt] schneiden 63

D

Dad [dæd] Papa 9
daffodils [ˈdæfədɪlz] die Osterglocken 120

daisy [ˈdeɪzɪ] das Gänseblümchen 119, 120
to dance [tə ˈdɑːns] tanzen 72
dangerous [ˈdeɪndʒərəs] gefährlich 106
dark [dɑːk] dunkel 55
dark blue [ˈdɑːk ˈbluː] dunkelblau 148, 152
daughter [ˈdɔːtə] die Tochter 9
day [deɪ] der Tag 55
December [dɪˈsembə] Dezember 125
to decorate [tə ˈdekəreɪt] schmücken 143
dentist [ˈdentɪst] der Zahnarzt, die Zahnärztin 37, 39
desk [desk] der Schreibtisch 25
dessert [dɪˈzɜːt] die Nachspeise 143
diary [ˈdaɪərɪ] das Tagebuch 120
dice [daɪs] der Würfel 22, 25
dictionary [ˈdɪkʃənrɪ] das Lexikon, das Wörterbuch 61, 63
difficult [ˈdɪfɪklt] schwierig 150
dining room [ˈdaɪnɪŋˌruːm] das Esszimmer 17
dinner (evening) [ˈdɪnə] das Abendessen 53, 55
dinosaur [ˈdaɪnəsɔː] der Dinosaurier 25
dirty [ˈdɜːtɪ] schmutzig 31, 150
to do [tə ˈduː] tun, machen 55
to do the gardening [tə ˈduː ðə ˈgɑːdnɪŋ] im Garten arbeiten 72
doctor [ˈdɒktə] der Arzt, die Ärztin 28, 31
dog [dɒg] der Hund 7, 9
dog food [ˈdɒgfuːd] das Hundefutter 79
doll [dɒl] die Puppe 22, 25

Wörterverzeichnis Englisch – Deutsch

dolphin ['dɒlfɪn] der Delfin **127**
door [dɔ:] die Tür **18**
down [daʊn] hinunter **153**
downstairs [ˌdaʊn'steəz] unten **18**
dragon ['drægən] der Drache (Fabelwesen) **70, 72**
to draw [tə 'drɔ:] zeichnen, malen **72**
to dream [tə 'dri:m] träumen **107**
dress [dres] das Kleid **47**
to dress up [tə ˌdres'ʌp] sich verkleiden **120**
dressing gown ['dresɪŋ ˌgaʊn] der Bademantel, der Morgenmantel **47**
drink [drɪŋk] das Getränk **79**
to drink [tə 'drɪŋk] trinken **79**
to drive [tə 'draɪv] fahren **93**
drum [drʌm] die Trommel **143**
dry [draɪ] trocken **150**
duck [dʌk] die Ente **99, 101**

E

ear [ɪə] das Ohr **28, 31**
earache ['ɪəreɪk] die Ohrenschmerzen **31**
early ['ɜ:lɪ] früh **39**
Easter ['i:stə] Ostern **120**
Easter bunny ['i:stəˌbʌnɪ] der Osterhase **119, 121**
Easter egg ['i:stər ˌeg] das Osterei **119, 121**
easy ['i:zɪ] einfach, leicht **150**
to eat [tʊ 'i:t] essen **73**
egg [eg] das Ei **76, 79**
eight [eɪt] acht **152**
eighteen [ˌeɪ'ti:n] achtzehn **152**
eighty ['eɪtɪ] achtzig **152**
elbow ['elbəʊ] der Ellenbogen **28, 31**
elephant ['elɪfənt] der Elefant **104, 107**
eleven [ɪ'levn] elf **152**
empty ['emptɪ] leer **151**

England ['ɪŋglənd] England **9**
English ['ɪŋglɪʃ] Englisch **9**
to enjoy [tə ɪn'dʒɔɪ] genießen **129**
entrance ['entrəns] der Eingang **86**
evening ['i:vnɪŋ] der Abend **55**
every ['evrɪ] jeden **93**
everywhere ['evrɪweə] überall **47**
excellent ['eksələnt] hervorragend, ausgezeichnet **39**
excuse me [ɪk'skju:z ˌmɪ] Entschuldigung! **107**
expensive [ɪk'spensɪv] teuer **151**
eye [aɪ] das Auge **32**
eyebrow ['aɪbraʊ] die Augenbraue **32**

F

face [feɪs] das Gesicht **32**
fairground ['feəgraʊnd] der Rummelplatz **115**
fairy ['feərɪ] die Fee **73**
to fall [tə 'fɔ:l] fallen **101**
to fall down [tə ˌfɔ:l'daʊn] hinfallen **32**
family ['fæmlɪ] die Familie **9**
famous ['feɪməs] berühmt **39**
farm [fɑ:m] der Bauernhof **101**
farmer ['fɑ:mə] der Bauer, die Bäuerin **101**
fast [fɑ:st] schnell **150**
fat [fæt] dick **150**
father ['fɑ:ðə] der Vater **6, 10**
Father Christmas (BE) ['fɑ:ðəˌkrɪsməs] der Weihnachtsmann **144**
favourite ['feɪvrət] Lieblings- **63**
February ['februərɪ] Februar **125**
to feed [tə 'fi:d] füttern **107**
to feel [tə 'fi:l] fühlen **32**
feet [fi:t] die Füße **32**

felt tip pen [felt ˌtɪp'pen] der Filzstift **60, 63**
fence [fens] der Zaun **98, 101**
field [fi:ld] das Feld **101**
fifteen [fɪf'ti:n] fünfzehn **152**
fifty ['fɪftɪ] fünfzig **152**
fine [faɪn] gut **10**
finger ['fɪŋgə] der Finger **32**
fire ['faɪə] das Feuer **144**
fire engine ['faɪərˌendʒɪn] das Feuerwehrauto **91, 93**
fire place ['faɪəpleɪs] der Kamin **140, 144**
fireworks ['faɪəwɜ:ks] das Feuerwerk **121**
first [fɜ:st] erste **115**
fish [fɪʃ] der Fisch **84, 87**
fishing [fɪʃɪŋ] Fischen **107**
five [faɪv] fünf **152**
flag [flæg] die Fahne, die Flagge **126, 129**
flat (BE) [flæt] die Wohnung **18**
floor [flɔ:] der Boden, Fußboden **25**
flour ['flaʊə] das Mehl **79**
flower ['flaʊə] die Blume **15, 18**
to fly [tə 'flaɪ] fliegen **129**
fog [fɒg] der Nebel **121**
food [fu:d] das Lebensmittel **79**
foot [fʊt] der Fuß **28, 32**
football ['fʊtbɔ:l] Fußball **71, 73**
forest ['fɒrɪst] der Wald **71, 73, 129**
to forget [tə fə'get] vergessen **121**
fork [fɔ:k] die Gabel **134, 137**
forty ['fɔ:tɪ] vierzig **152**
fountain ['faʊntɪn] der Brunnen **90, 93**
four [fɔ:] vier **152**
fourteen [ˌfɔ:'ti:n] vierzehn **152**
fox [fɒks] der Fuchs **98, 102**
France [frɑ:ns] Frankreich **129**
French [frentʃ] Französisch **63**

Wörterverzeichnis Englisch – Deutsch

Friday [ˈfraɪdeɪ] Freitag **125**
fridge [frɪdʒ] der Kühlschrank **80**
friend [frend] der Freund, die Freundin **6, 10**
friendly [frendlɪ] freundlich **39**
frog [frɒg] der Frosch **98, 102**
from [frɒm] von **153**
front door [ˌfrʌntˈdɔː] die Haustür **18**
frozen foods [ˌfrəʊznˈfuːdz] die Tiefkühlkost **87**
fruit [fruːt] das Obst **80, 87**
full [fʊl] voll **151**
fun [fʌn] der Spaß **39**
to have fun [tə hæv ˈfʌn] Spaß haben **115**
fur [fɜː] das Fell **107**

G

game [geɪm] das Spiel **22, 25**
garage [ˈgærɑːʒ] die Garage **18**
garden [ˈgɑːdn] der Garten **18**
geography [dʒɪˈɒgrəfɪ] Erdkunde **64**
German [ˈgɜːmən] Deutsch **10**
to get [tə ˈget] bekommen **137**
to get on [tə ˌgetˈɒn] einsteigen **93**
to get up [tə ˌgetˈʌp] aufstehen **53, 55**
ghost [gəʊst] das Gespenst, der Geist **112, 115**
ghost train [ˈgəʊst ˌtreɪn] die Geisterbahn **115**
giant [ˈdʒaɪənt] der Riese **70, 73**
giraffe [dʒɪˈrɑːf] die Giraffe **104, 107**
girl [gɜːl] das Mädchen **6, 10**
to give [tə ˈgɪv] geben, schenken **137**

glass [glɑːs] das Glas **134, 137**
glasses [ˈglɑːsɪz] die Brille **7, 10**
globe [gləʊb] der Globus **61, 64**
gloves [glʌvz] die Handschuhe **44, 47**
glue [gluː] der Klebstoff **60, 64**
to go [tə ˈgəʊ] gehen **115**
to go on holiday [tə gəʊ ɒn ˈhɒlədeɪ] in Urlaub fahren **129**
to go shopping [tə ˈgəʊ ˈʃɒpɪŋ] einkaufen gehen **87**
goal [gəʊl] das Fußballtor **73**
goal keeper [ˈgəʊl ˌkiːpə] der Torwart **70, 73**
goat [gəʊt] die Ziege **98, 102**
gold [ˈgəʊldən] golden **144**
good [gʊd] gut **151**
gorilla [gəˈrɪlə] der Gorilla **104, 107**
grandfather [ˈgrændˌfɑːðə] der Großvater **6, 10**
grandmother [ˈgrænˌmʌðə] die Großmutter **6, 10**
grandparents [ˈgrænˌpeərənts] die Großeltern **10**
grapes [greɪps] die Trauben **80**
grass [grɑːs] das Gras **18**
great [greɪt] toll **144**
Great Britain [ˈgreɪtˈbrɪtn] Großbritannien **64**
green [griːn] grün **148, 152**
green pepper [ˈgriːn ˈpepə] die grüne Paprikaschote **80**
grey (BE) [greɪ] grau **148, 152**
guitar [gɪˈtɑː] die Gitarre **70, 73**

H

hair [heə] das Haar **32**
hairbrush [ˈheəbrʌʃ] die Haarbürste **15, 18**
hall [hɔːl] der Flur **19**

Halloween [ˌhæləʊˈiːn] Halloween **121**
hamster [ˈhæmstə] der Hamster **61, 64**
hand [hænd] die Hand **32**
handbag [ˈhændbæg] die Handtasche **85, 87**
to hang [tə ˈhæŋ] hängen **47, 144**
happy [ˈhæpɪ] glücklich **39**
hard [hɑːd] hart **151**
hat [hæt] der Hut **48**
to hate [tə ˈheɪt] hassen **40**
to have [tə ˈhæv] haben **10**
he [hiː] er **153**
head [hed] der Kopf **33**
headache [ˈhedeɪk] die Kopfschmerzen **33**
to hear [tə ˈhɪə] hören **33**
heavy [ˈhevɪ] schwer **80, 152**
hedgehog [ˈhedʒhɒg] der Igel **98, 102**
helicopter [ˈhelɪkɒptə] der Hubschrauber **40**
hello [həˈləʊ] hallo **11**
help [tə ˈhelp] helfen **64**
helter skelter [ˌheltəˈskeltə] die Riesenrutsche **113, 115**
her [hɜː] ihr(e) **153**
hi [haɪ] hallo, hi **11**
to hide [tə ˈhaɪd] verstecken **40**
hide and seek [ˌhaɪdnˈsiːk] Verstecken **40**
hill [hɪl] der Hügel **102**
hippo [ˈhɪpəʊ] das Nilpferd **105, 108**
his [hɪz] sein(e) **153**
history [ˈhɪstrɪ] Geschichte **64**
hobby [ˈhɒbɪ] das Hobby **73**
to hold [tə ˈhəʊld] halten **108**
hole [həʊl] das Loch **48**
holiday [ˈhɒlədeɪ] der Urlaub **129**
holly [ˈhɒlɪ] die Stechpalme **141, 144**
homework [ˈhəʊmwɜːk] die Hausaufgaben **56**
honey [ˈhʌnɪ] der Honig **80**

Wörterverzeichnis Englisch – Deutsch

horrible [ˈhɒrəbl] schrecklich, grauenhaft 40
horse [hɔːs] das Pferd 99, 102
hospital [ˈhɒspɪtl] das Krankenhaus 93
hot [hɒt] heiß 129
hot chocolate [ˈhɒtˌtʃɒklət] die heiße Schokolade 80
hot dog [ˈhɒtdɒg] der Hotdog 115
hotel [ˌhəʊˈtel] das Hotel 126, 129
hour [aʊə] die Stunde 56
house [haʊs] das Haus 19
how [haʊ] wie 153
how many [ˈhaʊ ˈmenɪ] wie viele 153
to hug [tə ˈhʌg] umarmen 40
hungry [ˈhʌŋgrɪ] hungrig 40
to hurt [tə ˈhɜːt] wehtun 33
husband [ˈhʌzbənd] der Ehemann 11

I

I [aɪ] ich 153
I'm sorry [aɪm ˈsɒrɪ] es tut mir Leid 38
ice [aɪs] das Eis 144
ice cream [ˌaɪsˈkriːm] das Eis 134, 137
ice cream shop [ˈaɪskriːm ˌʃɒp] die Eisdiele 130
to ice skate [tʊ ˈaɪsˌskeɪt] Schlittschuh laufen 71, 73
idea [aɪˈdɪə] die Idee 130
ill [ɪl] krank 33
in [ɪn] in 153
in front of [ɪn ˈfrɒntˌɒv] vor 153
insect [ˈɪnsekt] das Insekt 108
inside [ˌɪnˈsaɪd] drinnen 153
interesting [ˈɪntrəstɪŋ] interessant 40
into [ˈɪntʊ] in, hinein 153
invitation [ˌɪnvɪˈteɪʃn] die Einladung 134, 138

to invite [tʊ ɪnˈvaɪt] einladen 138
is [ɪz] ist 11
island [ˈaɪlənd] die Insel 127, 130
it [ɪt] es 153
its [ɪts] sein(e) 153

J

jacket [ˈdʒækɪt] die Jacke 48
jam [dʒæm] die Marmelade 80
January [ˈdʒænjʊərɪ] Januar 125
jeans [dʒiːnz] die Jeans 48
jelly [ˈdʒelɪ] der Wackelpudding 134, 138
jellyfish [ˈdʒelɪfɪʃ] die Qualle 127, 130
joke [dʒəʊk] der Witz 40
juice [dʒuːs] der Saft 80
July [dʒuːˈlaɪ] Juli 125
to jump [tə ˈdʒʌmp] hüpfen, springen 115
jumper [ˈdʒʌmpə] der Pullover 44, 48
June [dʒuːn] Juni 125
jungle [ˈdʒʌŋgl] der Dschungel 108

K

kangaroo [ˌkæŋgəˈruː] das Känguru 108
to keep [tə ˈkiːp] halten, behalten 130
key [kiː] der Schlüssel 15, 19
keyboard [ˈkiːbɔːd] die Tastatur 22, 26
king [kɪŋ] der König 52, 56
to kiss [tə ˈkɪs] küssen 145
kitchen [ˈkɪtʃən] die Küche 19
kite [kaɪt] der Drache 118, 121
knee [niː] das Knie 29, 33
knife [naɪf] das Messer 134, 138
knight [naɪt] der Ritter 74
to know [tə ˈnəʊ] wissen, kennen 64

L

ladder [ˈlædə] die Leiter 14, 19
lamb [læm] das Lamm 99, 102
lamp [læmp] die Lampe 23, 26
language [ˈlæŋgwɪdʒ] die Sprache 65
last [lɑːst] letzte 116
late [leɪt] spät 40
to laugh [tə ˈlɑːf] lachen 36, 41
leaf [liːf] das Blatt 104, 108
to learn [tə ˈlɜːn] lernen 65
leaves [liːvz] die Blätter 108
left [left] links 94
leg [leg] das Bein 29, 33
lemon [ˈlemən] die Zitrone 76, 81
lemonade [ˌleməˈneɪd] die Limonade 138
lesson [ˈlesn] die Unterrichtsstunde 65
let's [lets] lass uns 108
letter [ˈletə] der Brief 94; der Buchstabe 65
letterbox [ˈletəbɒks] der Briefkasten 90, 94
lettuce [ˈletɪs] der Kopfsalat 85, 87
library [ˈlaɪbrərɪ] die Bücherei 41
lifeguard [ˈlaɪfgɑːd] der Rettungsschwimmer 127, 130
light [laɪt] hell, leicht 121, 152
light blue [ˈlaɪt ˈbluː] hellblau 148, 152
lighthouse [ˈlaɪthaʊs] der Leuchtturm 127, 130
lightning [ˈlaɪtnɪŋ] der Blitz 118, 121
to like [tə ˈlaɪk] mögen 41
to like doing something [tə ˈlaɪk ˈduɪŋ ˈsʌmθɪŋ] etwas gern tun 74

Wörterverzeichnis Englisch – Deutsch

lion [ˈlaɪən] der Löwe 105, 108
to listen to [tə ˈlɪsn‿tʊ] zuhören 74
to live [tə ˈlɪv] wohnen, leben 19
living room [ˈlɪvɪŋ‿ruːm] das Wohnzimmer 19
lizard [ˈlɪzəd] die Eidechse 108
long [lɒŋ] lang 150
to look [tə ˈlʊk] aussehen 33
to look for [tə ˈlʊk‿fɔː] suchen 19
lorry [ˈlɒrɪ] der Lastwagen 94
to lose [tə ˈluːz] verlieren 48
lots of [ˈlɒts ɒv] viele, eine Menge 145
loud [laʊd] laut 151
to love [tə ˈlʌv] lieben 41
lovely [ˈlʌvlɪ] schön 41
lunch [lʌntʃ] das Mittagessen 57
lunch break [ˈlʌntʃ‿breɪk] die Mittagspause 57

M

magazine [ˌmægəˈziːn] die Zeitschrift 87
magic [ˈmædʒɪk] die Zauberei 116
magic wand [ˈmædʒɪk ˈwɒnd] der Zauberstab 113, 116
magician [məˈdʒɪʃn] der Zauberer 113, 116
to make [tə ˈmeɪk] machen 65
to make a wish [tə ˈmeɪk ə ˈwɪʃ] sich etwas wünschen 138
man [mæn] der Mann 11
map [mæp] die Landkarte 61, 65
March [mɑːtʃ] März 125
market stall [ˈmɑːkɪtstɔːl] der Marktstand 91, 94
maths [mæθs] Mathematik 65
May [meɪ] Mai 125
maybe [ˈmeɪbiː] vielleicht 153
meat [miːt] das Fleisch 88
medicine [ˈmedsn] die Medizin, das Medikament 28, 33
melon [ˈmelən] die Melone 81
mess [mes] die Unordnung 48
mice [maɪs] die Mäuse 102
microwave [ˈmaɪkrəweɪv] die Mikrowelle 81
middle [ˈmɪdl] die Mitte 145
midnight [ˈmɪdnaɪt] Mitternacht 57
milk [mɪlk] die Milch 81
mine [maɪn] mein(e) 153
minute [ˈmɪnɪt] die Minute 57
mirror [ˈmɪrə] der Spiegel 29, 34
mistake [mɪˈsteɪk] der Fehler 65
mistletoe [ˈmɪsltəʊ] der Mistelzweig 140, 145
mobile phone [ˌməʊbaɪlˈfəʊn] das Handy 23, 26
Monday [ˈmʌndeɪ] Montag 125
money [ˈmʌnɪ] das Geld 85, 88
monkey [ˈmʌŋkɪ] der Affe 104, 109
monster [ˈmɒnstə] das Monster 112, 116
month [mʌnθ] der Monat 122
moon [muːn] der Mond 52, 57
morning [ˈmɔːnɪŋ] der Morgen, der Vormittag 57
mother [ˈmʌðə] die Mutter 7, 11
motorbike [ˈməʊtəbaɪk] das Motorrad 90
mouse [maʊs] die Maus 99, 102
mouse pad [ˈmaʊs‿pæd] das Mauspad 26
moustache [məˈstɑːʃ] der Schnurrbart 34
mouth [maʊθ] der Mund 28, 34
muddy [ˈmʌdɪ] dreckig 102
muesli [ˈmjuːzlɪ] das Müsli 81
mum [mʌm] Mama 11
mummy [ˈmʌmɪ] die Mumie 118, 122
museum [mjuːˈzɪːəm] das Museum 94
music [ˈmjuːzɪk] die Musik 74
my [maɪ] mein(e) 11

N

name [neɪm] der Name 11
neck [nek] der Hals 34
necklace [ˈnekləs] die Halskette 45, 48
to need [tə ˈniːd] brauchen 88
neighbour [ˈneɪbə] der Nachbar, die Nachbarin 19
nest [nest] das Nest 103
new [njuː] neu 151
New Year's Eve [ˌnjuːjɪəzˈiːv] Silvester 122
next [nekst] nächste(s) 116
next to [ˈnekst‿tʊ] neben 153
nice [naɪs] nett 81
night [naɪt] die Nacht 57
nine [naɪn] neun 152
nineteen [ˌnaɪnˈtiːn] neunzehn 152
ninety [ˈnaɪntɪ] neunzig 152
noisy [ˈnɔɪzɪ] laut 41
nose [nəʊz] die Nase 28, 34
to not feel well [tə ˈnɒt ˈfiːl ˈwel] sich unwohl fühlen 41
nothing [ˈnʌθɪŋ] nichts 41
November [nəʊˈvembə] November 125
numbers [ˈnʌmbəz] die Zahlen 152
nut [nʌt] die Nuss 77, 81

O

o'clock [əˈklɒk] … Uhr 122
October [ɒkˈtəʊbə] Oktober 125
of [ɒv] von 153

Wörterverzeichnis Englisch – Deutsch

of course [əfˈkɔːs] natürlich 109
off [ɒf] ab, aus 153
old [əʊld] alt 151
on [ɒn] auf 153
one [wʌn] eins 152
one hundred [ˌwʌnˈhʌndrəd] hundert 152
onion [ˈʌnjən] die Zwiebel 85, 88
open [ˈəʊpən] geöffnet 88
to open [tə ˈəʊpən] aufmachen, öffnen 145
opposite [ˈɒpəzɪt] gegenüber 153
opposites [ˈɒpəzɪts] die Gegensätze 150
or [ɔː] oder 153
orange [ˈɒrɪndʒ] orange 149, 152
orange [ˈɒrɪndʒ] die Orange 76, 81
orange juice [ˈɒrɪndʒ ˌdʒuːs] der Orangensaft 81
ouch [aʊtʃ] autsch, aua 34
our [ˈaʊə] unser(e) 153
outside [ˌaʊtˈsaɪd] draußen 153
over [ˈəʊvə] über 153
owl [aʊl] die Eule 99, 103

P

page [peɪdʒ] die Seite 65
to paint [tə ˈpeɪnt] malen 65
paintbrush [ˈpeɪntbrʌʃ] der Pinsel 60, 66
pair [peə] das Paar 48
pancake [ˈpænkeɪk] der Pfannkuchen 37, 41
panda [ˈpændə] der Panda 109
paper [ˈpeɪpə] das Papier 66
paper hat [ˈpeɪpə ˌhæt] der Papierhut 141, 145
pardon? [ˈpɑːdn] wie bitte? 109
parents [ˈpeərənts] die Eltern 11
park [pɑːk] der Park 94

parrot [ˈpærət] der Papagei 109
pavement [ˈpeɪvmənt] der Bürgersteig 94
paw [pɔː] die Pfote 109
to pay [tə ˈpeɪ] bezahlen 88
pea [piː] die Erbse 145
peacock [ˈpiːkɒk] der Pfau 105, 109
peanut butter [ˌpiːnʌt ˈbʌtə] die Erdnussbutter 81
pear [peə] die Birne 76, 82
pen [pen] der Stift 61, 66
pencil [ˈpensl] der Bleistift 61, 66
pencil case [ˈpensl ˌkeɪs] das Mäppchen 60, 66
pencil sharpener [ˈpensl ˌʃɑːpnə] der Bleistiftspitzer 60, 66
penguin [ˈpeŋgwɪn] der Pinguin 105, 109
people [ˈpiːpl] die Menschen, die Leute 116
pepper [ˈpepə] der Pfeffer 145
pet [pet] das Haustier 11
petrol (BE) [ˈpetrəl] das Benzin 95
petrol station (BE) [ˈpetrəlˌsteɪʃn] die Tankstelle 95
photo [ˈfəʊtəʊ] das Foto 12
to take photos [tə ˈteɪk ˈfəʊtəʊz] fotografieren 133
piano [pɪˈænəʊ] das Klavier 71, 74
to pick up [tə ˌpɪkˈʌp] aufheben 116
picnic [ˈpɪknɪk] das Picknick 130
pig [pɪg] das Schwein 98, 103
piggy bank [ˈpɪgɪbæŋk] das Sparschwein 23, 26
pillow [ˈpɪləʊ] das Kopfkissen 26
pilot [ˈpaɪlət] der Pilot 12
pineapple [ˈpaɪnæpl] die Ananas 82
pink [pɪŋk] rosa 149, 152

pirate [ˈpaɪrət] der Pirat 130
pizza [ˈpiːtsə] die Pizza 82
plane (aeroplane) [pleɪn] das Fleugzeug 131
plaster [ˈplɑːstə] das Pflaster 29, 34
plastic [ˈplæstɪk] das Plastik 88
plate [pleɪt] der Teller 135, 138
to play [tə ˈpleɪ] spielen 74
playground [ˈpleɪgraʊnd] der Spielplatz 95
please [pliːz] bitte 138
pocket [ˈpɒkɪt] die (Hosen)tasche 48
polar bear [ˌpəʊləˈbeə] der Eisbär 104, 109
police officer [pəˈliːsˌɒfɪsə] der Polizist, die Polizistin 95
pond [pɒnd] der Teich 95
poor [pɔː] arm 152
post office [ˈpəʊstˌɒfɪs] das Postamt 95
postcard [ˈpəʊstˌkɑːd] die Postkarte 126
poster [ˈpəʊstə] das Poster 23, 26
potato [pəˈteɪtəʊ] die Kartoffel 85, 88
to prefer [prɪˈfɜː] lieber mögen 146
present [ˈpreznt] das Geschenk 141, 146
prince [prɪns] der Prinz 74
princess [prɪnˈses] die Prinzessin 74
prize [praɪz] der Preis 116
problem [ˈprɒbləm] das Problem 49
puddle [ˈpʌdl] die Pfütze 122
to pull [tə ˈpʊl] ziehen 146
pumpkin [ˈpʌmkɪn] der Kürbis 118, 122
pupil [ˈpjuːpl] der Schüler, die Schülerin 66
purple [ˈpɜːpl] lila 149, 152
purse [pɜːs] der Geldbeutel 84, 88

161

Wörterverzeichnis Englisch – Deutsch

to push [tə 'pʊʃ] drücken, schieben **89**
to put [tə 'pʊt] stellen, setzen, legen **131**
to put away [tə ˌpʊt ə'weɪ] wegräumen **82**
pyjamas [pə'dʒɑːməz] der Schlafanzug **45, 49**

Q

queen [kwiːn] die Königin **52, 57**
question ['kwestʃən] die Frage **66**
queue [kjuː] die Menschenschlange **116**
quiet ['kwaɪət] ruhig, still, leise **95, 151**

R

rabbit ['ræbɪt] das Kaninchen **99, 103**
race ['reɪs] das Wettrennen **110**
radio ['reɪdɪəʊ] das Radio **23, 26**
rain [reɪn] der Regen **119, 122**
to rain [tə 'reɪn] regnen **122**
rainbow ['reɪnbəʊ] der Regenbogen **118, 122**
raincoat ['reɪnkəʊt] der Regenmantel **122**
raspberry ['rɑːzbəri] die Himbeere **82**
to read [tə 'riːd] lesen **12**
ready ['redɪ] bereit **110**
rectangle ['rektæŋgl] das Rechteck **153**
red [red] rot **149, 152**
reindeer ['reɪnˌdɪə] das Rentier **140, 146**
to relax [tə rɪ'læks] sich entspannen **131**
restaurant ['restərɒnt] das Restaurant **95**
rice [raɪs] der Reis **82**
rich [rɪtʃ] reich **152**
to ride [tə 'raɪd] reiten **110**

to ride a bike [tə 'raɪd ə 'baɪk] Rad fahren **70, 74**
right [raɪt] rechts **95**
right [raɪt] richtig **151**
to ring [tə 'rɪŋ] klingeln **66**
river ['rɪvə] der Fluss **90, 95**
to roar [tə 'rɔː] brüllen **110**
to roast [tə 'rəʊst] braten **146**
robin ['rɒbɪn] das Rotkehlchen **141, 146**
rock [rɒk] der Fels **131**
roll [rəʊl] das Brötchen **82**
roller coaster ['rəʊləˌkəʊstə] die Achterbahn **112, 117**
roller-blades ['rəʊləˌbleɪdz] die In-Liner **26**
roof [ruːf] das Dach **19**
room [ruːm] das Zimmer **26**
rose [rəʊz] die Rose **15, 20**
round [raʊnd] herum **153**
rubber (BE) ['rʌbə] der Radiergummi **67**
rucksack ['rʌksæk] der Rucksack **49**
ruler ['ruːlə] das Lineal **61, 67**
to run [tə 'rʌn] laufen **71, 74**

S

sack [sæk] der Sack **103**
sad [sæd] traurig **36, 41**
salad ['sæləd] der Salat **82**
salt [sɔːlt] das Salz **146**
sand [sænd] der Sand **131**
sandal ['sændl] die Sandale **49**
sandcastle ['sændˌkɑːsl] die Sandburg **126, 131**
sandwich ['sænwɪdʒ] das Sandwich **131**
Santa Claus (AE) ['sæntəklɔːz] der Weihnachtsmann **146**
Saturday ['sætədeɪ] Samstag **125**
sausage ['sɒsɪdʒ] das Würstchen **135, 139**
to say [tə 'seɪ] sagen **147**
scarecrow ['skeəkrəʊ] die Vogelscheuche **99, 103**

to be scared of [tə bɪ 'skeəd ɒv] Angst haben vor **38**
scarf [skɑːf] der Schal **44, 49**
school [skuːl] die Schule **67**
school holidays ['skuːlˌhɒlədeɪz] die Schulferien **123**
school playground ['skuːlˌpleɪgraʊnd] der Schulhof **67**
scissors ['sɪzəz] die Schere **61, 67**
to scratch [skrætʃ] kratzen **34**
sea [siː] das Meer **131**
seagull ['siːgʌl] die Möwe **127, 131**
seahorse ['siːhɔːs] das Seepferdchen **132**
seal [siːl] der Seehund **105, 110**
seashell ['siːʃel] die Muschel **127, 132**
season ['siːzn] die Jahreszeit **123**
to see [tə 'siː] sehen **34**
to sell [tə 'sel] verkaufen **96**
September [sep'tembə] September **125**
serviette [ˌsɜːvɪ'et] die Serviette **139**
seven [sevn] sieben **152**
seventeen [ˌsevn'tiːn] siebzehn **152**
seventy ['sevntɪ] siebzig **152**
shall [ʃæl] soll **49**
shampoo [ʃæm'puː] das Shampoo **15, 20**
shapes [ʃeɪps] die Formen **153**
shark [ʃɑːk] der Hai **132**
she [ʃiː] sie **153**
shed [ʃed] der Schuppen **20**
sheep [ʃiːp] das Schaf **98, 103**
shelf [ʃelf] das Regal **27**
shiny ['ʃaɪnɪ] glänzend **147**
ship [ʃɪp] das Schiff **127, 132**
shirt [ʃɜːt] das Hemd **49**
shoe [ʃuː] der Schuh **45, 49**
shop [ʃɒp] der Laden **96**

Wörterverzeichnis Englisch – Deutsch

shop assistant [ˈʃɒp‿əˌsɪstənt] der Verkäufer, die Verkäuferin 89
shopping bag [ˈʃɒpɪŋ‿bæg] die Einkaufstüte 82
shopping list [ˈʃɒpɪŋ‿lɪst] die Einkaufsliste 84, 89
short [ʃɔːt] kurz 150
shorts [ʃɔːts] die Shorts, die kurze Hose 49
shoulder [ˈʃəʊldə] die Schulter 34
show [ʃəʊ] die Vorstellung 117
to have a shower [tə hæv ə ˈʃaʊə] duschen 56
shower [ˈʃaʊə] die Dusche 20
sign [saɪn] das Schild 96
sign post [ˈsaɪnpəʊst] der Wegweiser 110
silver [ˈsɪlvə] silber 147
to sing [tə ˈsɪŋ] singen 71, 75
sink [sɪŋk] das Waschbecken 20
sister [ˈsɪstə] die Schwester 12
to sit [tə ˈsɪt] sitzen 27
to sit down [tə ˌsɪtˈdaʊn] sich hinsetzen 67
six [sɪks] sechs 152
sixteen [ˌsɪksˈtiːn] sechzehn 152
sixty [ˈsɪkstɪ] sechzig 152
skiing [ˈskiːɪŋ] Ski laufen 123
to skip [tə ˈskɪp] seilhüpfen 70, 75
skirt [skɜːt] der Rock 50
sky [skaɪ] der Himmel 123
to sleep [tə ˈsliːp] schlafen 53, 58
sleeping bag [ˈsliːpɪŋ‿bæg] der Schlafsack 36, 42
sleigh [sleɪ] der Schlitten 140, 147
to slide [tə ˈslaɪd] rutschen 117
slipper [ˈslɪpə] der Hausschuh 45, 50
slow [sləʊ] langsam 151
small [smɔːl] klein 150
smell [smel] Geruch 42
to smell [tə ˈsmel] riechen 42
to smile [tə ˈsmaɪl] lächeln 42
snake [sneɪk] die Schlange 105, 110
to sneeze [tə ˈsniːz] niesen 35
snow [snəʊ] der Schnee 147
snowball [ˈsnəʊbɔːl] der Schneeball 123
snowboard [ˈsnəʊbɔːd] das Snowboard 123
snowflake [ˈsnəʊfleɪk] die Schneeflocke 123
snowman [ˈsnəʊmæn] der Schneemann 141, 147
soap [səʊp] die Seife 15, 20
sock [sɒk] die Socke 44, 50
sofa [ˈsəʊfə] das Sofa 20
soft [sɒft] weich 151
something [ˈsʌmθɪŋ] etwas 42
sometimes [ˈsʌmtaɪmz] manchmal 27
son [sʌn] der Sohn 12
sore throat [ˈsɔː ˈθrəʊt] die Halsschmerzen 35
soup [suːp] die Suppe 82
sour [ˈsaʊə] sauer 150
spade [speɪd] die Schaufel 126, 132
spaghetti [spəˈgetɪ] die Spaghetti 77, 83
to speak [tə ˈspiːk] sprechen 12
spider [ˈspaɪdə] die Spinne 14, 20
to splash [tə ˈsplæʃ] spritzen 123
spoon [spuːn] der Löffel 135, 139
spring [sprɪŋ] der Frühling 125
square [skweə] das Quadrat 153
squirrel [ˈskwɪrəl] das Eichhörnchen 14, 20
stairs [steəz] die Treppe 20
stamp [stæmp] die Briefmarke 96
star [stɑː] der Stern 52, 58
starfish [ˈstɑːfɪʃ] der Seestern 127, 132
station [ˈsteɪʃn] der Bahnhof 96
to stay [tə ˈsteɪ] bleiben 132
to steal [tə ˈstiːl] stehlen 50
steps [steps] die Treppe 132
sticky [ˈstɪkɪ] klebrig 117
stocking [ˈstɒkɪŋ] der Strumpf 141, 147
stone [stəʊn] der Stein 132
to stop [tə ˈstɒp] anhalten 96
storm [stɔːm] der Sturm 123
story [ˈstɔːrɪ] die Geschichte 75
straight [streɪt] glatt 35
strawberry [ˈstrɔːberɪ] die Erdbeere 77, 83
street [striːt] die Straße 96
stripy [ˈstraɪpɪ] gestreift 50
subject [ˈsʌbdʒekt] das Fach 67
sugar [ˈʃʊgə] der Zucker 83
suitcase [ˈsuːtkeɪs] der Koffer 126, 133
summer [ˈsʌmə] der Sommer 125
sun [sʌn] die Sonne 123
Sunday [ˈsʌndeɪ] Sonntag 125
sunflower [ˈsʌnflaʊə] die Sonnenblume 118, 124
sunglasses [ˈsʌnˌglɑːsɪz] die Sonnenbrille 126, 133
sunny [ˈsʌnɪ] sonnig 124
suntan lotion [ˈsʌntænˌləʊʃn] die Sonnencreme 133
supermarket [ˈsuːpəˌmɑːkɪt] der Supermarkt 89
surfboard [ˈsɜːfbɔːd] Surfbrett 133
sweet [swiːt] der Bonbon 77, 83, 150
sweet [swiːt] süß 77, 83, 150
to swim [tə ˈswɪm] schwimmen 133
swimming costume [ˈswɪmɪŋˌkɒstjuːm] der Badeanzug 133

Wörterverzeichnis Englisch – Deutsch

swimming pool [ˈswɪmɪŋ‿puːl] das Schwimmbad **96**
swimming trunks [ˈswɪmɪŋ‿trʌŋks] die Badehose **133**
swing [swɪŋ] die Schaukel **91, 96**
sword [sɔːd] das Schwert **71, 75**

T

table [ˈteɪbl] der Tisch **139**
tablecloth [ˈteɪblklɒθ] das Tischtuch **139**
to take [tə ˈteɪk] nehmen **67**
to talk [tə ˈtɔːk] sprechen **35**
tap [tæp] der Wasserhahn **15, 21**
to taste [tə ˈteɪst] schmecken **42**
taxi [ˈtæksɪ] das Taxi **96**
tea [tiː] der Tee **83**
to teach [tə ˈtiːtʃ] unterrichten **67**
teacher [ˈtiːtʃə] der Lehrer, die Lehrerin **67**
team [ˈtiːm] die Mannschaft **75**
teddy bear [ˈtedɪ‿beə] der Teddybär **27**
teeth [tiːθ] die Zähne **52, 58**
telephone [ˈtelɪfəʊn] das Telefon **21**
telephone box [ˈtelɪfəʊn‿bɒks] die Telefonzelle **90, 97**
television [ˈtelɪvɪʒn] der Fernseher **14, 21**
to tell [tə ˈtel] erzählen **42**
ten [ten] zehn **152**
tennis [ˈtenɪs] das Tennis **75**
tennis ball [ˈtenɪs‿bɔːl] der Tennisball **27**
tennis player [ˈtenɪsˌpleɪə] der Tennisspieler, die Tennisspielerin **70, 75**
tennis racket [ˈtenɪsˌrækɪt] der Tennisschläger **22, 27**
tent [tent] das Zelt **36, 42**

test [test] die Klassenarbeit **68**
thank you [ˈθæŋk‿juː] Danke schön **139**
their [ðeə] ihr(e) **153**
they [ðeɪ] sie **153**
thin [θɪn] dünn **150**
thing [θɪŋ] das Ding **43**
to think [tə ˈθɪŋk] denken, glauben, meinen **89**
thirsty [ˈθɜːstɪ] durstig **43**
thirteen [ˌθɜːˈtiːn] dreizehn **152**
thirty [ˈθɜːtɪ] dreißig **152**
this [ðɪs] dies **12**
three [θriː] drei **152**
through [θruː] durch **153**
to throw [tə ˈθrəʊ] werfen **75**
thumb [θʌm] der Daumen **29, 35**
thunderstorm [ˈθʌndəstɔːm] das Gewitter **124**
Thursday [ˈθɜːzdeɪ] Donnerstag **125**
tick [tɪk] der Haken **68**
ticket [ˈtɪkɪt] die Fahrkarte **112, 117**
to tidy up [tə ˌtaɪdɪˈʌp] aufräumen **50**
tiger [ˈtaɪgə] der Tiger **110**
time [taɪm] die Zeit **58, 59**
timetable [ˈtaɪmˌteɪbl] der Stundenplan **68**
tin [tɪn] die Dose **84, 89**
tired [ˈtaɪəd] müde **43, 58**
to [tʊ/tə] zu **153**
toast [təʊst] der Toast **53, 58**
today [təˈdeɪ] heute **125**
toe [təʊ] der Zeh **29, 35**
toilet [ˈtɔɪlət] die Toilette **21**
toilet paper [ˈtɔɪlətˌpeɪpə] das Toilettenpapier **14, 21**
tomato [təˈmɑːtəʊ] die Tomate **77, 83**
tomorrow [təˈmɒrəʊ] morgen **125**
tonight [təˈnaɪt] heute Abend **58**
too [tuː] auch **12**
too many [ˈtuː ˈmenɪ] zu viele **43**

tooth [tuːθ] der Zahn **58**
toothache [ˈtuːθeɪk] die Zahnschmerzen **35**
toothbrush [ˈtuːθbrʌʃ] die Zahnbürste **53, 58**
toothpaste [ˈtuːθpeɪst] die Zahnpasta **53, 58**
tortoise [ˈtɔːtəs] die Schildkröte **6, 12**
towel [ˈtaʊəl] das Handtuch **21**
town [taʊn] die Stadt **97**
town hall [ˌtaʊnˈhɔːl] das Rathaus **97**
toy [tɔɪ] das Spielzeug **27**
tractor [ˈtræktə] der Traktor **103**
traffic [ˈtræfɪk] der Verkehr **97**
traffic lights [ˈtræfɪk‿laɪts] die Ampel **91, 97**
train [treɪn] der Zug **97**
trainers [ˈtreɪnəz] die Turnschuhe **44, 50**
tree [triː] der Baum **21**
tree house [ˈtriː‿haʊs] das Baumhaus **14**
triangle [ˈtraɪæŋgl] das Dreieck **153**
trolley [ˈtrɒlɪ] der Einkaufswagen **84, 89**
trousers [ˈtraʊzəz] die Hose **45, 51**
trunk [trʌŋk] der Rüssel **110**
to try on [tə ˌtraɪˈɒn] anprobieren **51**
T-shirt [ˈtiː‿ʃɜːt] das T-Shirt **51**
Tuesday [ˈtjuːzdɪ] Dienstag **125**
tummy [ˈtʌmɪ] der Bauch **35**
twelve [twelv] zwölf **152**
twenty [ˈtwentɪ] zwanzig **152**
twins [twɪnz] die Zwillinge **12**
two [tuː] zwei **152**

U

umbrella [ʌmˈbrelə] der Regenschirm **119, 124**
uncle [ˈʌŋkl] der Onkel **12**

Wörterverzeichnis Englisch – Deutsch

under [ˈʌndə] unter 153
to understand [tə ˌʌndəˈstænd] verstehen 110
underwear [ˈʌndəweə] die Unterwäsche 51
unicorn [ˈjuːnɪkɔːn] das Einhorn 111
uniform [ˈjuːnɪfɔːm] die Uniform 13
up [ʌp] hinauf, hoch 153
upstairs [ʌpˈsteəz] oben 21
to use [tə ˈjuːz] benutzen 68
usually [ˈjuːʒʊəlɪ] gewöhnlich, normalerweise 59

V

vampire [ˈvæmpaɪə] der Vampir 112, 117
vegetable [ˈvedʒtəbl] das Gemüse 89
very [ˈverɪ] sehr 139
very much [ˈverɪ ˈmʌtʃ] sehr 43
village [ˈvɪlɪdʒ] das Dorf 97

W

to wait [tə ˈweɪt] warten 117
to wake up [tə ˌweɪkˈʌp] aufwecken 59
walk [wɔːk] der Spaziergang 59
to walk [tə ˈwɔːk] zu Fuß gehen 59
wall [wɔːl] die Wand 27
to want [tə ˈwɒnt] wollen 43
wardrobe [ˈwɔːdrəʊb] der Kleiderschrank 44, 51
to wash [tə ˈwɒʃ] sich waschen 35
to wash the dishes [tə ˈwɒʃ ðə ˈdɪʃɪz] abspülen 43
watch [wɒtʃ] die Armbanduhr 45, 51
to watch [tə ˈwɒtʃ] beobachten 103
to watch TV [tə ˈwɒtʃ ˌtiːˈviː] fernsehen 59
water [ˈwɔːtə] das Wasser 83
watermelon [ˈwɔːtəˈmelən] die Wassermelone 83
to wave [tə ˈweɪv] winken 68
we [wiː] wir 153
to wear [tə ˈweə] tragen 51
weather [ˈweðə] das Wetter 124
Wednesday [ˈwenzdeɪ] Mittwoch 125
week [wiːk] die Woche 124
weekend [ˌwiːkˈend] das Wochenende 124
wet [wet] nass 150
whale [weɪl] der Wal 127, 133
what [wɒt] was 153
when [wen] wann 153
where [weə] wo 153
which [wɪtʃ] welche(r,-s) 153
to whisper [tə ˈwɪspə] flüstern 68
to whistle [tə ˈwɪsl] pfeifen 75
white [waɪt] weiß 149, 152
who [huː] wer 153
why [waɪ] warum 153
wife [waɪf] die Ehefrau 13
to win [tə ˈwɪn] gewinnen 117
wind [wɪnd] der Wind 124
window [ˈwɪndəʊ] das Fenster 27
winter [ˈwɪntə] der Winter 125
witch [wɪtʃ] die Hexe 112, 117
with [wɪð] mit 59, 153
woman [ˈwʊmən] die Frau 13
words [wɜːdʒ] die Wörter 68
world [wɜːld] die Welt 68
wrapping paper [ˈræpɪŋˌpeɪpə] das Geschenkpapier 139
to write [tə ˈraɪt] schreiben 68
wrong [rɒŋ] falsch 151

Y

year [jɪə] das Jahr 124
years old [ˈjɪəz ˈəʊld] Jahre alt 13
yellow [ˈjeləʊ] gelb 149, 152
yesterday [ˈjestədɪ] gestern 125
yoghurt [ˈjɒgət] der Joghurt 83
you [juː] du, ich, Sie 153
your [jɔː] dein(e), euer(e), Ihre(e) 153
yuck! [jʌk] Igitt! 111
yummy [ˈjʌmɪ] lecker 111

Z

zebra [ˈzebrə] das Zebra 111
zebra crossing [ˌzebrəˈkrɒsɪŋ] der Zebrastreifen 91, 97
zoo [zuː] der Zoo 111
zoo keeper [ˈzuːˌkiːpə] der Zoowärter 111

Wörterverzeichnis Deutsch – Englisch

A

ab off 153
Abend evening 55
Abendessen dinner 53, 55
aber but 153
abspülen to wash the dishes 43
acht eight 152
Achterbahn roller coaster 112, 117
achtzehn eighteen 152
achtzig eighty 152
Adresse address 16
Affe monkey 104, 109
Alphabet alphabet 62
alt old 151
Ameise ant 98
Ampel traffic lights 91, 97
an at 153
Ananas pineapple 82
anfangen to begin 54
Angst haben vor to be afraid of; to be scared of 38
anhalten to stop 96
anprobieren to try on 51
anstoßen to bump 30
Antwort answer 62
Apfel apple 76, 78
Apotheke chemist's 93
April April 125
Aquarium aquarium 106
Arm arm 29, 30
arm poor 152
Armband bracelet 46
Armbanduhr watch 45, 51
Arzt, Ärztin doctor 28, 31
Ast branch 104, 106
aua ouch 34
auch too 12
auf on 153
aufheben to pick up 116
aufmachen to open 145
aufräumen to tidy up 50
aufstehen to get up 53, 55
aufwecken to wake up 59
Auge eye 32
Augenbraue eyebrow 32
August August 125
aus off 153

ausblasen to blow out 136
ausgezeichnet excellent 39
aussehen to look 33
Auto car 92
Autoskooter bumper car 113, 114
autsch ouch 34

B

Baby baby 7, 8
backen to bake 136
Badeanzug swimming costume 133
Badehandtuch beach towel 128
Badehose swimming trunks 133
Bademantel dressing gown 47
baden to have a bath 33
Badewanne bath 16
Badezimmer bathroom 16
Bäckerei bakery 92
Bär bear 104, 106
Bahnhof station 96
Balkon balcony 16
Ball ball 22, 24
Banane banana 77, 78
Bank bank 92
Bart beard 7, 8
Baseball baseball 46
Basketball basketball 71, 72
Bauch tummy 35
bauen to build 128
Bauer, Bäuerin farmer 101
Bauernhof farm 101
Baum tree 21
Baumhaus tree house 14
behalten to keep 130
bei at 153
Bein leg 29, 33
beißen to bite 106
bekommen to get 137
bellen to bark 100
benutzen to use 68
Benzin petrol (BE) 95
beobachten to watch 103
bereit ready 110
berühmt famous 39
beschäftigt busy 72

besser better 38
beste, bester best 8
Bett bed 24
bewölkt cloudy 120
bezahlen to pay 88
Biene bee 14, 16
Bikini bikini 128
billig cheap 151
bin am 8
Birne pear 76, 82
bitte please 138
Blätter leaves 108
Blatt leaf 104, 108
blau blue 148, 152
blaue Fleck bruise 30
bleiben to stay 132
Bleistift pencil 61, 66
Bleistiftspitzer pencil sharpener 60, 66
Blitz lightning 118, 121
blond blonde 30
Blume flower 15, 18
Blumenkohl cauliflower 85, 86
Bluse blouse 46
bluten to bleed 30
Boden floor 25
Bohne bean 78
Bonbon sweet 77, 83, 150
Boot boat 128
braten to roast 146
brauchen to need 88
braun brown 148, 152
Brief letter 94
Briefkasten letterbox 90, 94
Briefmarke stamp 96
Brille glasses 7, 10
bringen to bring 46
Brötchen roll 82
Brot bread 84, 86
Bruder brother 8
Brücke bridge 90, 92
brüllen to roar 110
Brunnen fountain 90, 93
Brust chest 31
Buch book 60, 62
Buchstabe letter 65
Bücherei library 41
Bücherregal bookcase 62
Bürgersteig pavement 94
Burg castle 128

Wörterverzeichnis Deutsch – Englisch

Bus bus 91, 92
Busch bush 14, 17
Busfahrer, Busfahrerin bus driver 92
Bushaltestelle bus stop 90, 92
Butter butter 78

C

Café café 106
CD CD 24
CD-Player CD player 24
Chips crisps (BE) 77, 79
Clown clown 112, 114
Cola cola (coke®) 137
Comic-Heft comic 24
Computer computer 25
Computerspiel computer game 25
Cousin, Cousine cousin 9
Cowboy cowboy 113, 115

D

Dach roof 19
Dachboden attic 16
Danke schön thank you 139
Daumen thumb 29, 35
Decke blanket 46
dein(e) your 153
Delfin dolphin 127
denken to think 89
Deutsch German 10
Dezember December 125
dick fat 150
Dienstag Tuesday 125
dies this 12
Ding thing 43
Dinosaurier dinosaur 25
Donnerstag Thursday 125
Dorf village 97
Dose tin 84, 89
Drache kite 118, 121
Drache (Fabelwesen) dragon 70, 72
draußen outside 153
dreckig muddy 102
drei three 152
Dreieck triangle 153
dreizehn thirteen 152

dreißig thirty 152
drinnen inside 153
drücken to push 89
Dschungel jungle 108
du you 153
dünn thin 150
dunkel dark 55
dunkelblau dark blue 148, 152
durch through 153
durstig thirsty 43
Dusche shower 20
duschen to have a shower 56

E

Ecke corner 93
Ehefrau wife 13
Ehemann husband 11
Ei egg 76, 79
Eichhörnchen squirrel 14, 20
Eidechse lizard 108
Eimer bucket 99, 100
eine Menge lots of 145
einfach easy 150
Eingang entrance 86
Einhorn unicorn 111
einkaufen gehen to go shopping 87
Einkaufsliste shopping list 84, 89
Einkaufstüte shopping bag 82
Einkaufswagen trolley 84, 89
einladen to invite 138
Einladung invitation 134, 138
eins one 152
einsteigen to get on 93
Eis ice 144
Eis ice cream 134, 137
Eisbär polar bear 104, 109
Eisdiele ice cream shop 130
Elefant elephant 104, 107
elf eleven 152
Ellenbogen elbow 28, 31
Eltern parents 11
Engel angel 140, 142
England England 9
Englisch English 9
Ente duck 99, 101

Entschuldigung! excuse me 107
er he 153
Erbse pea 145
Erdbeere strawberry 77, 83
Erdkunde geography 64
Erdnussbutter peanut butter 81
Erkältung cold 31, 120
erste first 115
erste Weihnachtsfeiertag Christmas Day 143
erzählen to tell 42
es it 153
es tut mir Leid I'm sorry 38
essen to eat 73
Esszimmer dining room 17
etwas something 42
etwas gern tun to like doing something 74
euer(e) your 153
Eule owl 99, 103

F

Fach subject 67
Fahne flag 126, 129
fahren to drive 93
Fahrkarte ticket 112, 117
Fahrrad bicycle, bike 38
fallen to fall 101
falsch wrong 151
Familie family 9
fangen to catch 72
Farben colours 152
Februar February 125
Federball badminton 142
Fee fairy 73
Fehler mistake 65
feiern to celebrate 142
Feld field 101
Fell fur 107
Fels rock 131
Fenster window 27
fernsehen to watch TV 59
Fernseher television 14, 21
Feuer fire 144
Feuerwehrauto fire engine 91, 93
Feuerwerk fireworks 121
Filzstift felt tip pen 60, 63

167

Wörterverzeichnis Deutsch – Englisch

Finger finger 32
Fisch fish 84, 87
Fischen fishing 107
Flagge flag 126, 129
Flasche bottle 84, 86
Fledermaus bat 99, 100
Fleisch meat 88
Fleugzeug plane (aeroplane) 131
fliegen to fly 129
flüstern to whisper 68
Flur hall 19
Fluss river 90, 95
Formen shapes 153
Foto photo 12
Fotoapparat camera 126, 128
fotografieren to take photos 133
Frage question 66
fragen to ask 62
Frankreich France 129
Französisch French 63
Frau woman 13
Freitag Friday 125
Freund, Freundin friend 6, 10
freundlich friendly 39
frieren to be cold 120
Frosch frog 98, 102
früh early 39
Frühling spring 125
Frühstück breakfast 54
frühstücken to have breakfast 56
Fuchs fox 98, 102
fühlen to feel 32
fünf five 152
fünfzehn fifteen 152
fünfzig fifty 152
Füße feet 32
füttern to feed 107
Fuß foot 28, 32
Fußball football 71, 73
Fußballtor goal 73
Fußboden floor 25

G

Gabel fork 134, 137
Gänseblümchen daisy 119, 120
Garage garage 18

Garten garden 18
Gebäude building 92
geben to give 137
Geburtstag birthday 136
Geburtstagsgeschenk birthday present 135, 136
Geburtstagskarte birthday card 135, 136
Geburtstagskuchen birthday cake 134, 136
Geburtstagsparty birthday party 136
gefährlich dangerous 106
Gegensätze opposites 150
gegenüber opposite 153
gehen to go 115
Geist ghost 112, 115
Geisterbahn ghost train 115
gelb yellow 149, 152
Geld money 85, 88
Geldbeutel purse 84, 88
Gemüse vegetable 89
genießen to enjoy 129
geöffnet open 88
Geruch smell 42
Geschenk present 141, 146
Geschenkpapier wrapping paper 139
Geschichte history 64; story 75
geschlossen closed 86
Gesicht face 32
Gespenst ghost 112, 115
gestern yesterday 125
gestreift stripy 50
Getränk drink 79
gewinnen to win 117
Gewitter thunderstorm 124
gewöhnlich usually 59
Giraffe giraffe 104, 107
Gitarre guitar 70, 73
glänzend shiny 147
Glas glass 134, 137
glatt straight 35
glauben to believe 38; to think 89
Globus globe 61, 64
Glocke bell 60, 62
glücklich happy 39
golden gold 144
Gorilla gorilla 104, 107

Gras grass 18
grau grey (BE) 148, 152
grauenhaft horrible 40
groß big 150
Großbritannien Great Britain 64
Großeltern grandparents 10
Großmutter grandmother 6, 10
Großvater grandfather 6, 10
grün green 148, 152
grüne Paprikaschote green pepper 80
Gürtel belt 45, 46
gut fine 10; good 151

H

Haar hair 32
Haarbürste hairbrush 15, 18
haben to have 10
hängen to hang 47, 144
Hai shark 132
hallo hello, hi 11
Halloween Halloween 121
Hals neck 34
Halskette necklace 45, 48
Halsschmerzen sore throat 35
halten to hold 108; to keep 130
Hamster hamster 61, 64
Hand hand 32
Handschuhe gloves 44, 47
Handtasche handbag 85, 87
Handtuch towel 21
Handy mobile phone 23, 26
hart hard 151
hassen to hate 40
Haus house 19
Hausaufgaben homework 56
Hausschuh slipper 45, 50
Haustier pet 11
Haustür front door 18
Heiligabend Christmas Eve 143
heiß hot 129
heiße Schokolade hot chocolate 80
heißen to be called 8
helfen help 64

168

Wörterverzeichnis Deutsch – Englisch

hell light 121
hellblau light blue 148, 152
Hemd shirt 49
Herbst autumn 125
herum round 153
hervorragend excellent 39
heute today 125
heute Abend tonight 58
Hexe witch 112, 117
hi hi 11
Himbeere raspberry 82
Himmel sky 123
hinauf up 153
hinein into 153
hinfallen to fall down 32
hinter behind 153
Hintern bottom 30
hinunter down 153
Hobby hobby 73
hoch up 153
Höhle cave 128
hören to hear 33
Honig honey 80
Hose trousers 45, 51
(Hosen)tasche pocket 48
Hotdog hot dog 115
Hotel hotel 126, 129
Hubschrauber helicopter 40
Hügel hill 102
Hüpfburg bouncy castle 112, 114
hüpfen to jump 115
Huhn chicken 98, 100
Hund dog 7, 9
Hundefutter dog food 79
hundert one hundred 152
hungrig hungry 40
Husten cough 31
Hut hat 48

I

ich I 153
Idee idea 130
Igel hedgehog 98, 102
Igitt! yuck! 111
ihr(e) her 153
ihr(e) their 153
Ihr(e) your 153
im Garten arbeiten to do the gardening 72
immer always 54
in in 153
in into 153
in Urlaub fahren to go on holiday 129
In-Liner roller-blades 26
Insekt insect 108
Insel island 127, 130
interessant interesting 40
irgendein(e) any 114
irgendwelche any 114
ist is 11

J

Jacke jacket 48
Jahr year 124
Jahre alt years old 13
Jahreszeit season 123
Januar January 125
Jeans jeans 48
jeden every 93
Joghurt yoghurt 83
Juli July 125
Junge boy 7, 8
junge Hahn cockerel 99, 101
Juni June 125

K

Käfig cage 61, 63
Känguru kangaroo 108
Käse cheese 76, 78
Kaffee coffee 79
Kalender calendar 119, 120
kalt cold 31, 120
Kamel camel 105, 106
Kamin fire place 140, 144
Kaninchen rabbit 99, 103
kaputt machen to break 24
Karotte carrot 86
Kartoffel potato 85, 88
Karussell carousel 113, 114
Kassette cassette 24
Kater cat 7, 8
Katze cat 7, 8
kaufen to buy 86
Keks biscuit 78
Keller cellar 17
kennen to know 64
Kerze candle 135, 137
Kind child 9
Kinder children 9
Kinn chin 31
Kino cinema 93
Kirche church 93
Klassenarbeit test 68
Klassenzimmer classroom 63
Klavier piano 71, 74
klebrig sticky 117
Klebstoff glue 60, 64
Kleid dress 47
Kleiderbügel clothes hanger 44, 47
Kleiderschrank wardrobe 44, 51
Kleidung clothes 47
klein small 150
klettern to climb 9
klingeln to ring 66
klug clever 39
Knallbonbon Christmas cracker 140, 142
Knie knee 29, 33
Knochen bone 28, 30
Knopf button 45, 46
kochen to cook 72
König king 52, 56
Königin queen 52, 57
können can 17, 63
Körper body 30
Koffer suitcase 126, 133
kommen to come 55
kommen aus to come from 9
Kopf head 33
Kopfkissen pillow 26
Kopfsalat lettuce 85, 87
Kopfschmerzen headache 33
Korb basket 77, 78
Krabbe crab 126, 128
krank ill 33
Krankenhaus hospital 93
Krankenwagen ambulance 91, 92
kratzen to scratch 34
Kreide chalk 63
Kreis circle 153
Krokodil crocodile 105, 106
Krone crown 53, 55
Kuchen cake 142

Wörterverzeichnis Deutsch – Englisch

Küche kitchen 19
Kühlschrank fridge 80
Küken chick 100
Kürbis pumpkin 118, 122
küssen to kiss 145
Kuh cow 99, 101
Kunde, Kundin customer 86
Kunst art 62
kurz short 150
kurze Hose shorts 49

L

lachen to laugh 36, 41
Laden shop 96
lächeln to smile 42
Lamm lamb 99, 102
Lampe lamp 23, 26
Land countryside 17, 101
Landkarte map 61, 65
Landschaft countryside 17, 101
lang long 150
langsam slow 151
langweilig boring 39
lass uns let's 108
Lastwagen lorry 94
laufen to run 71, 74
laut noisy 41; loud 151
leben to live 19
Lebensmittel food 79
lecker yummy 111
leer empty 151
legen to put 131
Lehrer, Lehrerin teacher 67
leicht easy 150; light 152
leise quiet 95, 151
Leiter ladder 14, 19
lernen to learn 65
lesen to read 12
letzte last 116
Leuchtturm lighthouse 127, 130
Leute people 116
Lexikon dictionary 61, 63
lieben to love 41
lieber mögen to prefer 146
Lieblings- favourite 63
lila purple 149, 152
Limonade lemonade 138
Lineal ruler 61, 67

links left 94
Loch hole 48
lockig curly 31
Löffel spoon 135, 139
Löwe lion 105, 108
Luftballon balloon 134, 136

M

machen to do 55; to make 65
Mädchen girl 6, 10
Mäppchen pencil case 60, 66
März March 125
Mäuse mice 102
Mai May 125
Mais corn 101
malen to paint 65
malen to draw 72
Mama mum 11
manchmal sometimes 27
Mann man 11
Mannschaft team 75
Mantel coat 47
Marktstand market stall 91, 94
Marmelade jam 80
Mathematik maths 65
Maus mouse 99, 102
Mauspad mouse pad 26
Medikament medicine 28, 33
Medizin medicine 28, 33
Meer sea 131
Mehl flour 79
mein(e) my 11; mine 153
meinen to think 89
Melone melon 81
Menschen people 116
Menschenschlange queue 116
Messer knife 134, 138
Mikrowelle microwave 81
Milch milk 81
Minute minute 57
Mistelzweig mistletoe 140, 145
mit with 59, 153
Mittagessen lunch 57
Mittagspause lunch break 57
Mitte middle 145

Mitternacht midnight 57
Mittwoch Wednesday 125
mögen to like 41
Möwe seagull 127, 131
Monat month 122
Mond moon 52, 57
Monster monster 112, 116
Montag Monday 125
Morgen morning 57
morgen tomorrow 125
Morgenmantel dressing gown 47
Motorrad motorbike 90
müde tired 43, 58
Mülleimer bin 114
Müsli muesli 81
Mütze cap 46
Mumie mummy 118, 122
Mund mouth 28, 34
Muschel seashell 127, 132
Museum museum 94
Musik music 74
Mutter mother 7, 11

N

nach after 54
Nachbar, Nachbarin neighbour 19
Nachmittag afternoon 54
Nachspeise dessert 143
Nacht night 57
nächste(s) next 116
Name name 11
Nase nose 28, 34
nass wet 150
natürlich of course 109
Nebel fog 121
neben next to 153
nehmen to take 67
Nest nest 103
nett nice 81
neu new 151
neun nine 152
neunzehn nineteen 152
neunzig ninety 152
nichts nothing 41
niesen to sneeze 35
Nilpferd hippo 105, 108
noch mal again 114
normalerweise usually 59

Wörterverzeichnis Deutsch – Englisch

November November 125
Nuss nut 77, 81

O

oben upstairs 21
Obst fruit 80, 87
oder or 153
öffnen to open 145
Ohr ear 28, 31
Ohrenschmerzen earache 31
Oktober October 125
Onkel uncle 12
orange orange 149, 152
Orange orange 76, 81
Orangensaft orange juice 81
Osterei Easter egg 119, 121
Osterglocken daffodils 120
Osterhase Easter bunny 119, 121
Ostern Easter 120

P

Paar pair 48
Panda panda 109
Papa Dad 9
Papagei parrot 109
Papier paper 66
Papierhut paper hat 141, 145
Park park 94
Parkbank bench 91, 92
Pause break 62
Pfannkuchen pancake 37, 41
Pfau peacock 105, 109
Pfeffer pepper 145
pfeifen to whistle 75
Pferd horse 99, 102
Pflaster plaster 29, 34
Pfote paw 109
Pfütze puddle 122
Picknick picnic 130
Pilot pilot 12
Pinguin penguin 105, 109
Pinsel paintbrush 60, 66
Pirat pirate 130
Pizza pizza 82
Plastik plastic 88

Plumpudding Christmas pudding 141, 143
Po bottom 30
Polizist, Polizistin police officer 95
Postamt post office 95
Poster poster 23, 26
Postkarte postcard 126
Preis prize 116
Prinz prince 74
Prinzessin princess 74
Problem problem 49
Pullover jumper 44, 48
Puppe doll 22, 25

Q

Quadrat square 153
Qualle jellyfish 127, 130

R

Rad fahren to ride a bike 70, 74
Radiergummi rubber (BE) 67
Radio radio 23, 26
Rathaus town hall 97
Rechteck rectangle 153
rechts right 95
Regal shelf 27
Regen rain 119, 122
Regenbogen rainbow 118, 122
Regenmantel raincoat 122
Regenschirm umbrella 119, 124
regnen to rain 122
reich rich 152
Reis rice 82
reiten to ride 110
Rentier reindeer 140, 146
Restaurant restaurant 95
Rettungsschwimmer lifeguard 127, 130
richtig right 151
riechen to smell 42
Riese giant 70, 73
Riesenrad big wheel 113
Riesenrutsche helter skelter 113, 115
Ritter knight 74

Rock skirt 50
rosa pink 149, 152
Rose rose 15, 20
rot red 149, 152
Rotkehlchen robin 141, 146
Rucksack rucksack 49
Rücken back 30
Rüssel trunk 110
ruhig quiet 95, 151
Rummelplatz fairground 115
rutschen to slide 117

S

Sack sack 103
Saft juice 80
sagen to say 147
Sahne cream 79
Salat salad 82
Salz salt 146
sammeln to collect 72
Samstag Saturday 125
Sand sand 131
Sandale sandal 49
Sandburg sandcastle 126, 131
Sandwich sandwich 131
sauber clean 150
sauer sour 150
Schachtel box 22, 24
Schaf sheep 98, 103
Schal scarf 44, 49
Schale bowl 78
Schaufel spade 126, 132
Schaukel swing 91, 96
schenken to give 137
Schere scissors 61, 67
Scheune barn 100
schieben to push 89
Schiff ship 127, 132
Schild sign 96
Schildkröte tortoise 6, 12
Schlafanzug pyjamas 45, 49
schlafen to sleep 53, 58
Schlafsack sleeping bag 36, 42
Schlafzimmer bedroom 16
Schlange snake 105, 110
schlau clever 39
schlecht bad 151
schließen to close 106

171

Wörterverzeichnis Deutsch – Englisch

Schlitten sleigh 140, 147
Schlittschuh laufen to ice skate 71, 73
Schloss castle 128
Schlüssel key 15, 19
schmecken to taste 42
Schmetterling butterfly 98, 100
schmücken to decorate 143
schmutzig dirty 31, 150
Schnee snow 147
Schneeball snowball 123
Schneeflocke snowflake 123
Schneemann snowman 141, 147
schneiden to cut 63
schnell fast 150
Schnurrbart moustache 34
schön beautiful 38; lovely 41
Schokolade chocolate 76, 78
Schornstein chimney 15, 17
Schrank cupboard 79
schrecklich horrible 40
schreiben to write 68
Schreibtisch desk 25
Schüler, Schülerin pupil 66
Schüssel bowl 78
Schuh shoe 45, 49
Schule school 67
Schulferien school holidays 123
Schulhof school playground 67
Schulter shoulder 34
Schuppen shed 20
schwarz black 148, 152
Schwein pig 98, 103
schwer heavy 80, 152
Schwert sword 71, 75
Schwester sister 12
schwierig difficult 150
Schwimmbad swimming pool 96
schwimmen to swim 133
sechs six 152
sechzehn sixteen 152
sechzig sixty 152
Seehund seal 105, 110
Seepferdchen seahorse 132
Seestern starfish 127, 132
sehen to see 34

sehr very 139; very much 43
Seife soap 15, 20
seilhüpfen to skip 70, 75
sein to be 8
sein(e) his; its 153
Seite page 65
September September 125
Serviette serviette 139
Sessel armchair 14, 16
setzen to put 131
Shampoo shampoo 15, 20
Shorts shorts 49
sich die Zähne putzen to brush one's teeth 54
sich entspannen to relax 131
sich etwas wünschen to make a wish 138
sich hinsetzen to sit down 67
sich unwohl fühlen to not feel well 41
sich verkleiden to dress up 120
sich waschen to wash 35
sie she; they 153
Sie you 153
sieben seven 152
siebzehn seventeen 152
siebzig seventy 152
silber silver 147
Silvester New Year's Eve 122
sind are 8
singen to sing 71, 75
sitzen to sit 27
Ski laufen skiing 123
Snowboard snowboard 123
Socke sock 44, 50
Sofa sofa 20
Sohn son 12
soll shall 49
Sommer summer 125
Sonne sun 123
Sonnenblume sunflower 118, 124
Sonnenbrille sunglasses 126, 133
Sonnencreme suntan lotion 133
sonnig sunny 124
Sonntag Sunday 125

spät late 40
Spaghetti spaghetti 77, 83
Sparschwein piggy bank 23, 26
Spaß fun 39
Spaß haben to have fun 115
Spaziergang walk 59
Spiegel mirror 29, 34
Spiel game 22, 25
spielen to play 74
Spielplatz playground 95
Spielzeug toy 27
Spinne spider 14, 20
Sprache language 65
sprechen to speak 12; to talk 35
springen to jump 115
spritzen to splash 123
Stadt town 97
Stechpalme holly 141, 144
stehlen to steal 50
Stein stone 132
stellen to put 131
Stern star 52, 58
Stiefel boots 44, 46
Stift pen 61, 66
still quiet 95
Strand beach 128
Straße street 96
Strauch bush 14, 17
Strumpf stocking 141, 147
Stuhl chair 23, 24
Stunde hour 56
Stundenplan timetable 68
Sturm storm 123
suchen to look for 19
süß sweet 77, 83, 150
Supermarkt supermarket 89
(Supermarkt-) Kasse check-out 86
Suppe soup 82
Surfbrett surfboard 133

T

T-Shirt T-shirt 51
Tafel blackboard 62
Tag day 55
Tagebuch diary 120
Tankstelle petrol station (BE) 95

Wörterverzeichnis Deutsch – Englisch

Tante aunt 8
tanzen to dance 72
Tasche bag 46
Taschenrechner calculator 61, 63
Tasse cup 135, 137
Tastatur keyboard 22, 26
Taxi taxi 96
Teddybär teddy bear 27
Tee tea 83
Teich pond 95
Telefon telephone 21
Telefonzelle telephone box 90, 97
Teller plate 135, 138
Tennis tennis 75
Tennisball tennis ball 27
Tennisschläger tennis racket 22, 27
Tennisspieler, Tennisspielerin tennis player 70, 75
Teppich carpet 17
teuer expensive 151
Tiefkühlkost frozen foods 87
Tier animal 100
Tiger tiger 110
Tisch table 139
Tischtuch tablecloth 139
Toast toast 53, 58
Tochter daughter 9
Toilette toilet 21
Toilettenpapier toilet paper 14, 21
toll great 144
Tomate tomato 77, 83
Torwart goal keeper 70, 73
träumen to dream 107
tragen to wear 51; to carry 78
Traktor tractor 103
Trauben grapes 80
traurig sad 36, 41
Treppe stairs 20; steps 132
trinken to drink 79
trocken dry 150
Trommel drum 143
Tür door 18
tun to do 55
Turnschuhe trainers 44, 50

U

über about; over; above 153
überall everywhere 47
Uhr clock 52, 55
... Uhr o'clock 122
um about 153
umarmen to hug 40
und and 153
Uniform uniform 13
Unordnung mess 48
unser(e) our 153
unten downstairs 18
unter below; under 153
unterrichten to teach 67
Unterrichtsstunde lesson 65
Unterwäsche underwear 51
Urlaub holiday 129

V

Vampir vampire 112, 117
Vater father 6, 10
Verband bandage 29, 30
vergessen to forget 121
Verkäufer, Verkäuferin shop assistant 89
verkaufen to sell 96
Verkehr traffic 97
verlieren to lose 48
verstecken to hide 40
Verstecken hide and seek 40
verstehen to understand 110
viele lots of 145
vielleicht maybe 153
vier four 152
vierzehn fourteen 152
vierzig forty 152
Vogel bird 100
Vogelhäuschen bird house 15, 17
Vogelscheuche scarecrow 99, 103
voll full 151
von from, of 153
vor before 54; in front of 153
Vorhang curtain 14, 17
Vormittag morning 57
Vorstellung show 117

W

Wackelpudding jelly 134, 138
Wal whale 127, 133
Wald forest 71, 73, 129
Wand wall 27
wann when 153
warten to wait 117
warum why 153
was what 153
Waschbecken sink 20
Wasser water 83
Wasserhahn tap 15, 21
Wassermelone watermelon 83
Wecker alarm clock 23, 24
wegräumen to put away 82
Wegweiser sign post 110
wehtun to hurt 33
weich soft 151
Weihnachten Christmas 142
Weihnachtsbaum Christmas tree 140, 143
Weihnachtskarte Christmas card 142
Weihnachtslied Christmas carol 142
Weihnachtsmann Father Christmas (BE) 144
Weihnachtsmann Santa Claus (AE) 146
weil because 153
weinen to cry 39
weiß white 149, 152
welche(r,-s) which 153
Welt world 68
wer who 153
werfen to throw 75
Wetter weather 124
Wettrennen race 110
wie as; how 153
wie bitte? pardon? 109
wie viele? how many? 153
Wind wind 124
winken to wave 68
Winter winter 125
wir we 153
wissen to know 64
Witz joke 40

Wörterverzeichnis Deutsch – Englisch

wo where 153
Woche week 124
Wochenende weekend 124
Wörter words 68
Wörterbuch dictionary 61, 63
wohnen to live 19
Wohnung apartment (AE) 16; flat (BE) 18
Wohnzimmer living room 19
Wolke cloud 118, 120
wollen to want 43
Würfel dice 22, 25
Würstchen sausage 135, 139
wütend angry 38

Z

Zähne teeth 52, 58
Zahlen numbers 152
Zahn tooth 58
Zahnarzt, Zahnärztin dentist 37, 39
Zahnbürste toothbrush 53, 58
Zahnpasta toothpaste 53, 58
Zahnschmerzen toothache 35
Zauberei magic 116
Zauberer magician 113, 116
Zauberstab magic wand 113, 116
Zaun fence 98, 101
Zebra zebra 111
Zebrastreifen zebra crossing 91, 97
Zeh toe 29, 35
zehn ten 152
zeichnen to draw 72
Zeit time 58, 59
Zeitschrift magazine 87
Zelt tent 36, 42
Ziege goat 98, 102
ziehen to pull 146
Zimmer room 26
Zitrone lemon 76, 81
Zoo zoo 111
Zoowärter zoo keeper 111
zu to; at 153
zu Fuß gehen to walk 59
zu Hause at home 16
zu viele too many 43
Zucker sugar 83
Zuckerwatte candy floss 113, 114
Zug train 97
zuhören to listen to 74
zumachen to close 106
zustimmen to agree 38
zwanzig twenty 152
zwei two 152
Zwiebel onion 85, 88
Zwillinge twins 12
zwischen between 153
zwölf twelve 152